DISCARDED

CONFEDERATE CENTENNIAL STUDIES

WM. STANLEY HOOLE, *Editor-in-Chief*

Number *Ten*

HOWELL COBB'S CONFEDERATE CAREER

By

HORACE MONTGOMERY

MAJOR-GENERAL HOWELL COBB, C. S. A.
(Courtesy, University of Georgia Library, Athens)

Howell Cobb's Confederate Career

By
HORACE MONTGOMERY

CONFEDERATE PUBLISHING COMPANY, INC.
TUSCALOOSA   1959   ALABAMA

LIMITED EDITION

Only four hundred and fifty copies of this book have been printed, after which the type was destroyed.

PRINTED IN THE UNITED STATES OF AMERICA BY SWS PRINTERS, 410 GREENSBOBO AVENUE, TUSCALOOSA, ALABAMA

To
Timothy Thomas Montgomery
A Great Comfort and Delight
Do I Dedicate this Book.

Contents

Foreword

Howell Cobb's public career spanned more than a quarter of a century. Among the honors accorded him were speaker of the United States House of Representatives, governor of Georgia, and secretary of the United States Treasury. He actively sought, but failed to win, the Democratic nomination for the presidency in 1860. Soon after the Republican victory of that year he returned to Georgia and helped to take his state out of the Union. In the hectic days that followed, he reached what he considered the summit of his public career, when he was chosen *de facto* President of the Confederate States of America. Early in the War for Southern Independence he chose a military career and rose to the rank of major-general. A prodigious worker and methodical public servant, Cobb was also a talented conciliator.

However, because he lacked the luster of some of his contemporaries, he has received slight notice from historians. While this monograph is principally concerned with his military career, it also presents his role in the events that immediately preceded the war. Its author hopes that it will bring long-due credit to a far from ordinary man, about whom so little is known.

Among the numerous persons who have rendered valuable assistance in the preparation of this monograph, I am especially grateful to Will Erwin, a grandson of Howell Cobb, John W. Bonner, Jr., and Susan B. Tate, Special Collections librarian and library assistant, Special Collections Division, respectively, at the University of Georgia Library. To E. Merton Coulter, Bell Irvin Wiley, and T.

Harry Williams I express my thanks for their generous interruptions of busy teaching and writing schedules to read the manuscript. Each has made numerous helpful suggestions, but to the shortcomings of this work, whatever they are, I lay exclusive claim.

Athens, Georgia   HORACE MONTGOMERY
Winter, 1958

HOWELL COBB'S CONFEDERATE CAREER

CHAPTER I

First Leader of the Confederacy

A "FAT, PUSSY, ROUND-FACED, jolly looking fellow" was the way an Alabama newsman described the presiding officer of the Confederate Provisional Congress, meeting in Montgomery during the early part of 1861.[1] The object of this not altogether complimentary observation was Howell Cobb of Athens, Georgia, who had learned to accept such remarks in good humor. Before the Congress was to adjourn he found it necessary to be in New Orleans for a few days. While there he stopped in a barber shop. His barber, described by Cobb as a Creole, glanced at him and inquired whether there were no barbers where he came from. Cobb replied stoutly in the affirmative, whereupon the Creole, running a hand over his customer's countenance, remarked: "By gar, you are a fat one. I be tam—but he fat." In relating the incident to his wife on March 5, Cobb seemed to enjoy the barber's amusement.[2]

Late in 1860 Cobb quit President James Buchanan's Cabinet to lead a spirited campaign to take Georgia out of the Union. For eighteen years (1842-1860) he had been in state and national politics—ten years in the Congress, one two-year term as governor, and almost four years as secretary of the Treasury. Until shortly before he left that post, he had been conspicuous for his efforts in defense of both the national Democratic party and the Federal

---

[1] Huntsville (Ala.) *Southern Democrat*, Feb. 20, 1861.
[2] This letter, as well as other manuscripts cited, unless otherwise indicated, are in the privately-owned Cobb Collection and used with kind permission of Mr. Will Erwin of Athens, Ga.

Union.   Indeed, at mid-century his name was synonymous with "unionism."

Born at Cherry Hill, Jefferson County, Georgia on September 7, 1815, Howell was the oldest child of John Addison Cobb and Sara Rootes Cobb.   During his youth his parents had moved to Athens where he was to enter Franklin College (now the University of Georgia).   About a year after his graduation in 1834 he married seventeen-year-old Mary Ann Lamar, daughter of a wealthy Milledgeville merchant-planter.   In 1836 he was admitted to the bar. He quickly proved himself a talented lawyer and the next year the legislature chose him solicitor general of the state's western circuit.[3]

Cobb's rise in state and national politics was rapid.   In 1842 he was elected to Congress on the general ticket.   He quickly learned the rudiments of parliamentary maneuver and became a valued leader and staunch defender of the Democratic party.[4]   Re-elected three consecutive times by the sixth district, the Georgian was a veteran legislator when the 31st Congress opened in December, 1849.   After a protracted contest he was declared speaker on the sixty-third ballot.   Senator John C. Calhoun bitterly observed that Cobb's Northern colleagues had chosen him, because of all Southerners he was the least loyal to the Southern viewpoint.[5]

Speaker Cobb immediately found himself in the midst of the fight over Henry Clay's Omnibus Bill.   Adopted to save the Union, the measure became known as the Compromise of 1850.   Extremists grumbled about it, and in

[3] A sketch of Cobb's career to 1860 may be found in John Savage, *Our Living Representative Men* (Philadelphia, 1860), 114-127; another, to 1849, in *United States Magazine, and Democratic Review,* XXV, 266-276 (Sept., 1849) ; and some materials are in the Erwin Collection (University of Georgia Library, Athens). See also Zachary T. Johnson, *Political Policies of Howell Cobb* (Nashville, 1929) and Samuel Boykin (ed.), *Memorial Volume of Hon. Howell Cobb of Georgia* (Philadelphia, 1870).

[4] See Cobb's "Necessity for Party Organization," *Congressional Globe,* 30 Cong., 1 Sess., 775-779 (July 1, 1848).

[5] Nathan Sargent, *Public Men and Events* (Philadelphia, 1875), II, 353; Johnson, 82-83; Charles M. Wiltse, *John C. Calhoun, Sectionalist, 1840-1850* (Indianapolis, 1951), 452.

Georgia its friends were apprehensive. When the governor ordered a convention to decide whether Georgia should accept it, Cobb and several of his colleagues hastened home to convince Georgians of the wisdom of recent congressional action. In the process Cobb broke with the regular Democratic party in Georgia and joined with certain Whigs to put over the Compromise. Once the state convention had endorsed the legislation, its Georgia supporters organized the Union party. In 1851 it nominated Cobb for governor; he easily defeated the candidate of the regular Democrats.[6]

Now scorned by Georgia's regular Democrats, Governor Cobb's position became exceedingly precarious after they succeeded in getting control of the state party machine during the winter of 1851-1852. Cobb was still young and ambitious. He believed his future lay with the Democrats, rather than the makeshift Union party. He must therefore make peace with the regular Democratic party chieftains. Waiting until shortly after the inauguration of President Franklin Pierce, for whom he had actively campaigned, Cobb publicly recanted in March, 1853. Union party leaders at once excoriated him, while regular Democrats strongly denied there had been a genuine conversion.[7]

Cobb hoped to settle the issue of his party loyalty by supporting the Democratic candidate for governor in 1853. His effort may have been the decisive factor in a very close race. Feeling that his reaffirmation of faith in his old party was now beyond challenge, soon after he left the governor's office he entered the contest for the Democratic nomination for United States senator. Badly beaten, he returned to the practice of law.[8]

Unable to win reinstatement at the hands of his state's party leaders, Cobb decided to try at the national level.

[6] Robert P. Brooks, "Howell Cobb and the Crisis of 1850," *Mississippi Valley Historical Review*, IV, 279-298 (Dec., 1917); Horace Montgomery, *Cracker Parties* (Baton Rouge, 1950), 17-44.
[7] Horace Montgomery (ed.), *Georgians in Profile* ... (Athens, 1958), 217-218.
[8] Montgomery, *Cracker Parties*, 117-119.

For this reason, he wrote his wife on December 23,[9] he had
entered the race for his old seat in Congress. He easily
defeated his Know Nothing opponent, and within three
weeks after the opening of the 34th Congress he was convinced that his mission had already been accomplished.
He had won reinstatement in the national Democratic party,
he explained, by taking the floor of Congress and delivering
a speech acclaiming that party as the nation's best hope.[10]

Despite the conquest he claimed to have made in Washington, Cobb had not yet been forgiven at home, and John
E. Ward, the influential Savannah politician who had recently presided at the Democratic national convention, so
informed him. He wrote Cobb a "private and confidential"
letter, July 5, 1856, on the eve of the presidential contest,
expressing his belief that the former governor was now
less popular in his own state and section than anywhere
else in the country.[11]

Cobb was paying dearly for having taken leave of the
Democratic preserve in 1850-1851. But he was as determined as ever to win from Georgia party leaders and
Southern Democrats generally the absolution he had been
seeking since his repentance of early 1853. Ahead of him
was the presidential contest of 1856. A deft performance
in behalf of his party might turn the trick. His friend
James Buchanan, the Pennsylvania "doughface," had already been nominated by the Democrats, and the newly
organized Republican party, committed to the doctrine
of non-extension of slavery, had presented John C. Fremont
as its first presidential candidate. Cobb took the field for
Buchanan, campaigning actively in Pennsylvania and In-
diana, keeping a close watch on the South. Although he
had earlier accepted the abstract right of secession, he now
boldly declared he would favor the secession of Georgia in
the event of a Republican victory.[12]

[9] Ulrich B. Phillips (ed.), *Correspondence of Robert Toombs, Alexander Stephens, and Howell Cobb* (Washington, 1913), 356.
[10] Quoted in Robert P. Brooks, "Howell Cobb Papers," *Georgia
Historical Quarterly*, VI, 157-158 (Dec., 1922).
[11] Phillips, 372-373.
[12] Johnson, 148, 169; Montgomery, *Cracker Parties*, 42.

The presidential election of 1856 enabled Cobb to accomplish two things. It gave him the opportunity to endorse the ultimate in Southern rights, which he believed would assure his acceptance by the Democratic leaders of his state, and it placed President-elect Buchanan heavily in his debt. The Pennsylvanian was to express his gratitude by naming Cobb Secretary of the Treasury. The Georgia Democrats were to wait three years and then, when support from home was to be essential to his progress within the national party, they were to reiterate their deep-seated contempt for him by withholding endorsement for the Democratic nomination for the presidency.

Partly because President Buchanan was a bachelor and Secretary of State Lewis Cass an elderly man, the Cobb home became the center of Washington social life during the years immediately before the Civil War.[13] The Cobbs were a hospitable couple and they injected a measure of gaiety into public affairs at a time when violence prevailed in Kansas and disaster was threatening the nation's economy.

Cobb's influence in the Cabinet was not limited to the Treasury Department. As the leading Southerner in the administration, he was the South's spokesman on slavery and, consequently, he became deeply involved in the President's bitter fight with Senator Stephen A. Douglas of Illinois. During the Senator's campaign for re-election in 1858 against Republican Abraham Lincoln, Cobb privately expressed a strong distrust of and an intense personal distaste for Douglas. He may have preferred a Republican victory in Illinois in 1858. It would have eliminated Douglas and given Cobb greater freedom in tipping the Democratic party more decisively southward. Cobb believed this was necessary to contain the growing extremism below the Potomac and to deter the rising Republican party.[14]

The Douglas victory did not make things easier for

---

[13] Elizabeth Mays, " 'The Celebrated Mrs. Cobb'—Mrs. Howell Cobb," *Georgia Historical Quarterly*, XXIV, 101-122 (June, 1940).
[14] Cobb to Stephens, Sept. 8, 1858 (Phillips, 442-444).

President Buchanan and his Secretary of the Treasury. The latter grew increasingly pessimistic. Just before Congress met in December, 1859, he privately expressed to Alexander H. Stephens his serious misgivings concerning the South's future, stating that only the nomination of a Southerner for President in 1860 could forestall disaster. This may have been Cobb's way of letting Stephens know he was about to make a bid for his party's nomination.[15] At any rate, one week after he had written Stephens, some of Cobb's supporters in the legislature met in Milledgeville and ordered a state convention for December 8. The next day the state Democratic executive committee ordered another convention for March. The December convention, alleged by many party leaders to have been highly irregular, met and agreed to put Cobb in the race for the party's nomination for President at Charleston.[16]

After heated local contests between Cobb and anti-Cobb factions, delegates were finally selected to attend the March convention. These contests must have convinced Cobb that he had not been forgiven for his aberration of 1850-1851. Assembling on March 14, the delegates promptly rescinded the action of the December convention. Whatever chance Cobb had had of winning his party's nomination for the presidency now vanished.[17]

The story of the Democracy's preparation for the presidential contest of 1860 is a dismal record of strident behavior, bolting delegates, splinter conventions and, finally, a complete schism between the party's Northern and Southern components. The former nominated Douglas, the latter John C. Breckinridge. Other contenders were Abraham Lincoln, the Republican nominee, who campaigned on the principle of non-extension of slavery, and John Bell, the Constitutional Union party's nominee, who urged his countrymen not to break up the Union over slavery.

Cobb canvassed Georgia for Breckinridge, appearing in Columbus, Athens, Dalton, and other places. The South's

[15] Cobb to Stephens, Nov. 14, 1859 (Phillips, 448-559).
[16] Montgomery, *Cracker Parties*, 237.
[17] Cobb to John B. Lamar, Jan. 15, 1860 (Phillips, 456-457).

position, he contended, was the true constitutional position. He believed Douglas a dangerous man. Lincoln was even worse and, if he were elected, Cobb thought the South "ought" to secede and he was convinced it "would" do so.[18] Cobb's sanguinity as to Breckinridge's prospects was not shared by his friends and relatives. Their letters abound with references to the lack of interest in Breckinridge's election.[19] The returns confirmed these gloomy reflections, for Breckinridge was able to poll only a minority of Georgia's popular votes and in Clarke County, Cobb's home, he was badly beaten by Bell.[20] Neither of these candidates won the presidency, however; that prize went to Abraham Lincoln.

For Howell Cobb the outcome of the election of 1860 brought immediate torture. Although pledged to secession, he felt a duty to his old friend President Buchanan. He revealed something of his anguish in a letter, written November 16, to his brother-in-law, John B. Lamar of Macon. Buchanan, he insisted, was the South's true friend and to abandon him in his hour of greatest trial would be "unworthy and disgraceful." On the other hand, he confessed that he could not long remain a member of the administration. He was planning to make his report to Congress and then issue an "address" to the people of Georgia, reviewing the hopeless state of affairs and urging immediate secession as the only remedy. He would go to the President and explain that his duty to Georgia and to himself required such an "address." Afterwards he hoped to leave the administration with "good feeling."

While Cobb was in Washington wrestling with his conscience, officials in Georgia were preparing to meet the

---

[18] See Cobb to James Jackson, Nov. 1, to John B. Lamar, Oct. 31, to Mrs. Cobb, Oct. 10, 1860; Johnson, 162-163.
[19] L. Whittle to John B. Lamar, Sept. 22, John A. Cobb to his mother, Oct. 1, A. R. Lawton to Cobb, Nov. 5, T. R. R. Cobb to Cobb, Nov. 5, 1860.
[20] The vote, as reported by the Milledgeville (Ga.) *Federal Union*, Nov. 27, 1860, was Breckinridge, 51,893, Bell 42, 886, Douglas, 11, 580. (This paper later became the *Southern Federal Union.*) The Clarke County vote, as reported by the Athens (Ga.) *Southern Banner*, Nov. 8, 1860, was Bell, 695, Breckinridge, 541, Douglas, 57.

crisis Lincoln's victory had produced. On November 7, the day after the election, the legislature, still uncertain of the winner, convened, and on the following day Governor Joseph E. Brown informed the lawmakers that, if the "Black Republicans" were declared victorious, he would recommend a state convention. On November 17 the legislators ordered the convention delegates to be chosen in each county on January 2 and to convene two weeks later in the state capital.

Meanwhile, Cobb was approaching the termination of his Washington connections. On December 1 he promised his brother-in-law that his "address" would appear shortly. Finished five days later, it proved to be a sixteen-page pamphlet designed to stir the people of Georgia to immediate secession.[21] It was weighted with complaints, forebodings, and generous quotations from the clamorous rhetoric of leading Republicans. Cobb handed it to Attorney General Jeremiah S. Black for delivery to President Buchanan and sent copies home for publication in the newspapers. On December 8 he wrote Buchanan he was leaving the Cabinet, giving strong assurance that he was taking such action out of no resentment toward the President.[22] Two days later Buchanan acknowledged receipt of Cobb's letter of resignation. He commended the Georgian for having run an efficient department and wished a different decision had been possible, "because our relations have ever been of the most friendly and confidential character."

Shortly before mid-December Cobb was on his way to Georgia. He stopped in Columbia, South Carolina, where earlier there had been talk of getting Georgia to take the lead in seceding.[23] However, this project was abandoned in favor of a short-lived scheme for Georgia and South Carolina to secede jointly.[24] Apparently, Cobb was plan-

[21] *Ibid.*, Dec. 20, 1860; Phillips, 505-516.
[22] Cobb to his wife, Dec. 7, to Buchanan, Dec. 8, 1860 (Phillips, 517-518).
[23] John B. Lamar to David C. Barrow, Dec. 13, 1860 (in Barrow Papers, University of Georgia Library, Athens).
[24] W. H. G. (?) to William P. Miles, Nov. 8, 1860 (in Miles Papers, University of North Carolina Library, Chapel Hill); John B. Lamar to David C. Barrow, Dec. 8, 1860 (Barrow Papers).

ning to promote such a joint effort, but in Columbia he received instructions from Governor Brown and a group of Southerners still in Washington, urging him to let South Carolina act alone.[25] Immediately, Cobb went on to Georgia.

At home in Athens he found the Secessionists beset with forebodings. With only two weeks remaining in the campaign to elect delegates, everything seemed to be going against them.[26] Most distressing to their cause was the spate of public meetings which warned against hasty action and in some instances even denied that Lincoln's election was reason enough for breaking up the Union.[27] Such gatherings were most numerous in Cobb's district. At first he considered asking the voters of one of his counties to elect him as a delegate, but, fearing defeat, he abandoned the idea.[28] Instead, he undertook an intensive speaking tour of North Georgia.[29] From that hilly region he wrote his wife on December 26 and 29 that in some of the counties he had found "submission" sentiment overwhelming, but assured her "a great change was made." One observer claimed that "he stirs up the hearts of people . . . and they show how they are affected by their cheers."[30]

Whether South Carolina's secession on December 20 softened resistance to Cobb among his old Unionist friends cannot be ascertained, but the election on January 2 indicated they were strongly opposed to breaking up the Union.[31] Although the state-wide voting resulted in the election of a majority of delegates, who were finally to support immediate secession, many North Georgia counties chose complete slates of Unionists who expected to go to the

[25] Lamar to Barrow, Dec. 13, 1860 (Barrow Papers); Cobb to his wife, Dec. 10, Brown to Cobb, Dec. 15, 1860; William H. Trescott to Cobb, Dec. 14, 1860 (Phillips, 522).
[26] T. R. R. Cobb to Cobb, Dec. 8, 15, John B. Cobb to Cobb, Dec. 14, 1860.
[27] A number of meetings were reported in the *Southern Banner*, Dec. 13, 20, 1860.
[28] Cobb to his wife, Dec. 26, 1860.
[29] See *Southern Banner*, Dec. 20, 1860, for his itinerary.
[30] J. B. Guthrie to Phillip Clayton, Dec. 27, 1860.
[31] See Herbert Fielder, *A Sketch of the Life and Times and Speeches of Joseph E. Brown* (Springfield, 1883), 174-177, for the vote on the secession ordinance.

convention two weeks later and record their convictions.[32] However, some of the Secessionist leaders persisted in the hope that many of the latter would vote for secession once they got to the convention, if beforehand they were "properly tutored" and "attended to."[33] To secure such "uncoerced consent," Cobb continued his relentless drive against Unionism.[34]

Less than one week before the Georgia State Constitutional Convention met, Cobb privately expressed the hope that the South would be able to get "a *peaceable* and *perpetual* separation."[35] It was extremely important, therefore, that the convention take Georgia out of the Union promptly and with a minimum of bickering. This called for some well-laid plans, which were carefully worked out at the home of John B. Lamar. For weeks Lamar's home had been a "hotbed of secession" and it was now the meetplace of a group that was preparing "a program" for the convention.[36] Cobb assisted in formulating this program. He was able to do so because Lamar, who was a delegate from Bibb County, was accustomed to following Cobb's advice on important political matters. Moreover, Cobb was in close touch with South Carolina and for the guidance of the Macon planners obtained copies of the resolutions and ordinances already adopted by that state's secession convention.[37]

Georgians have long regarded the body of men who sat briefly in their Capitol in mid-January, 1861 as their most distingushed political assemblage. Although Cobb was not a member, he and Governor Brown, along with some other notables, were given seats on the floor on January 14.[38]

[32] *Federal Union*, Jan. 8, 1861; Johnson, 170-172.
[33] Andrew Young to Cobb, Jan. 4, 1861.
[34] *Southern Banner*, Jan. 9, 1861.
[35] Cobb to William P. Miles, Jan. 10, 1861 (Miles Papers).
[36] Mrs. Cobb to Cobb, Dec. 10, 1860, H. L. Benning to John B. Lamar, John Milton to John B. Lamar, Jan. 11, 1861.
[37] Cobb to William P. Miles, Jan. 10, 1861 (Miles Papers) ; Miles to Cobb, Jan. 14, 1861 (Phillips, 528-529).
[38] *Journal of the Public and Secret Proceedings of the Convention of the People of Georgia . . .* (Milledgeville, 1861), 13.

On the nineteenth, Cobb wired his son, Lamar, that the Ordinance of Secession had been adopted. Georgia was now out of the Union. Cobb's role in taking it out had been an important one. A friend was later to claim that had "he advised otherwise or had he been silent, it is universally believed that Georgia would not have seceded when she did; and had she declined to secede, . . . it is also universally believed that the other States would not have seceded."[39] Although such an extravagant assertion cannot be supported, it can be said that, if Howell Cobb had opposed secession, the seceders would have had a harder fight.

A few days after it adopted the secession ordinance, the Georgia convention chose delegates to the proposed congress of seceded states which was to meet on February 4 at Montgomery, Alabama. Ten was the number agreed upon, one from each of the eight congressional districts and two from the state at large.[40] Among the former was Alexander H. Stephens; chosen for the latter were Robert Toombs and Howell Cobb. For ten years these three men had been the most prominent figures in Georgia politics. They gave real distinction to the Georgia delegation which T. R. R. (Tom) Cobb, Howell's younger brother and also a delegate, believed to be the most powerful at Montgomery.[41] Unionists a decade earlier, all three men were destined to assist mightily in the formation of the Confederate States of America.

According to prearrangement, the Provisional Congress, the first session of which is sometimes called the Montgomery Convention, met on February 4.[42] Delegates from South Carolina, Florida, Alabama, Mississippi, and Louisi-

[39] Boykin, 30; Alexander H. Stephens, *A Constitutional View of the Late War Between the States* . . . (Philadelphia, 1870), II, 332.
[40] See *ibid.*, II, 322-325; *Southern Federal Union*, Jan. 29, 1861.
[41] T. R. R. Cobb to his wife, Feb. 4, 1861 (in T. R. R. Cobb Letters, University of Georgia Library, Athens). This collection is hereinafter cited as Cobb Letters.
[42] There were five sessions of the Confederate Congress, Feb. 4, 1861-Feb. 14, 1862. The first two met in Montgomery, the last three in Richmond. Cobb presided over all of them, although he was in the Confederate States Army after July, 1861.

ana joined Georgia's ten men to begin the work of organizing a government. On motion of South Carolina's R. B.
Rhett, Howell Cobb was unanimously chosen to serve as
president of the Congress. In a short acceptance speech
Cobb sought to dispel doubt, excite hope, and move the
timid to action. Separation from the old Union, he assured
his listeners, was "perfect, complete, and perpetual." He
urged that a cordial welcome be extended to the late sister
states, whose interests were identical with those of the
states represented at Montgomery. With the remainder of
the states of the old Union and with the world at large the
embryonic Confederacy must remain at peace. In con-
clusion, Cobb predicted that the delegates were about to
inaugurate "for the South a new era of peace, security,
and prosperity."[43]

Howell Cobb was particularly well suited for the role of
president of the Provisional Congress. A man of immense
prestige, he had been secretary of the United States Treasury only two months before the Montgomery gathering.
To entrust one of his stature with the responsibility of
presiding at the new nation's birth would demonstrate the
determination of the delegates. Moreover, Cobb was a
negotiator—his reputation as a politician rested largely
on this special talent. In the trying days just ahead many
looked to him to manage things in such a way as to over-
come opposition to secession in Maryland, Virginia, North
Carolina, and elsewhere.[44] Because he had many friends
among Northern Democrats, there was a chance they would
help him to avoid a collision with the incoming Lincoln
administration. Of all the Confederate leaders, Cobb was
best suited for such a delicate maneuver and to the very
last he believed war could be averted.[45]

[43] *Journal of the Congress of the Confederate States of America,
1861-1865* (Washington, 1904-1905), I, 16.
[44] Levi K. Bowers to Cobb, March 14, R. M. T. Hunter to Cobb,
March 15, 1861.
[45] Philip Clayton to Cobb, Feb. 8, 11, Junius Hillyer to Cobb, Feb. 9,
11, Cobb to Mrs. Cobb, May 5, 15, 1861; Cobb to his wife, March 28,
1861 (Cobb Folder, University of Georgia Library, Athens).

Although all of these considerations were involved in the decision to accord Howell Cobb the distinction of becoming the Confederacy's first leader, the evidence strongly suggests that he may have received the honor primarily as a result of what must be construed as petty politics. Many Southerners had not forgiven Cobb for his behavior in the early 1850's. Distrustful of him now, they saw in the presidency of the Provisional Congress a means of withholding from him a much more important prize, the presidency of the Confederacy itself, which was to be awarded within a week. In a letter to his wife, February 3, Cobb strongly denied he had been the victim of such intrigue, but many of his friends believed otherwise.[46]

Once the Provisional Congress had completed its organization, it moved rapidly, adopting rules of procedure, approving a temporary constitution for the six Confederate States of America and, on February 9, choosing provisional officers.[47] Although there was some sentiment for placing Cobb in the presidency, there was considerably more for Jefferson Davis of Mississippi, who was unanimously elected. In like manner, Alexander H. Stephens became Vice-President.[48] On February 18 Cobb administered the oath of office to President Davis.

Cobb was pleased with the choice of Davis, but the election of Stephens was a bitter disappointment. He privately boasted that only he himself could have changed the outcome of that contest. A man of intense pride, he may have felt that he had rendered sufficient service to the Southern cause to justify his choice as the new nation's President. Denied the important office, he wanted no such "empty compliment" as the vice-presidency. Indeed, his private correspondence justifies the belief that he had as much contempt for this office as he did for the man who

[46] Phillips, 536-537.
[47] Stephens, II, 328.
[48] E. Merton Coulter, *Confederate States of America* (Baton Rouge, 1950), 25; John Milton to John B. Lamar, Jan. 22, 1861; William H. Trescott to William P. Miles, Feb. 6, 1861 (Miles Papers).

was to fill it.[49]   Yet he was not unappreciative of the
argument that Stephens' election was a much-needed ges-
ture to Unionists. Everywhere they were strong. In the
border states they were holding back secession; in North
Georgia they were restive; and even in Alabama, according
to the confession of one Secessionist, there were enough of
them to carry the state for reunion.[50]

After the election of officers, the Congress tackled the
important problem of drafting a permanent constitution.
Prepared in approximately four weeks, it was adopted on
March 11. The next day Cobb explained to a friend, George
W. Crawford, that the new document departed from the
United States Constitution only where necessary to guard
against what were considered the dangers and evils "which
led to the dissolution of the late Union."[51]

Before the Congress adjourned on March 16, President
Cobb commended the members for their hard work, recalling that the daily sessions had sometimes lasted nine hours.
Their discussions, he continued, had always been honest,
able, and relevant. To have presided over such a body was
a signal honor. Believing that their crowning achievement
was the Constitution of the Confederate States of America,
he boastfully concluded that it was the "ablest ever prepared . . . for a free people."[52]

[49] Cobb to John A. Cobb, Feb. 10, 15, 1861.
[50] J. W. H. Underwood to Cobb, Feb. 1, Levi K. Bowers to Cobb,
March 14, W. P. Mount to John B. Lamar, March 31, 1861; A. R.
Wright to Cobb, Feb. 1, 1861 (Phillips, 536).
[51] Allen D. Candler (ed.), *Confederate Records of the State of
Georgia* (Atlanta, 1909-1911), I, 705-706.
[52] *Journal of the Congress*, I, 152.

Chapter II

Statesman and Soldier

SHORTLY AFTER CONGRESS ADJOURNED, Cobb attended a Masonic gathering in New Orleans, his second trip to that city since the first of the year. On the night of April 1 he was awakened in his room in the St. Charles Hotel by the sound of martial music in the street. Upon investigating, he discovered the Louisiana Guards were serenading him. He responded with an address, writing his wife the following day that, inasmuch as no reporters had been present, he would be spared "the mortification of reading that speech in print."

While in New Orleans Cobb called on John Slidell who, as United States senator from Louisiana, had been friendly to him and to other members of President Buchanan's Cabinet. What the two men discussed is not known, but Slidell had previously written Cobb that he had been "especially intimate" with Count Henri Mercier, the French minister in Washington, and did not doubt that Louis Napoleon would recognize the Confederacy at an early date. He had insisted that France, rather than England, was the key to the Confederacy's relations with Europe and concluded "in strict confidence" by writing Cobb on February 13 that he would like to be considered for the post of minister to France.

A few days later President Davis invited Slidell to serve with James M. Mason as a commissioner to Europe. Slidell's immediate reaction to the offer was one of petulance. He notified Cobb of the offer, explaining ". . . as between ourselves, if there had been no other objection the association with Mason would have been sufficient to decide my declension." He expressed a complete lack of faith in commissions. He was a believer, he continued, in "one man power" and would go to Paris because he could be useful, but he would not share with another either the responsibility of a failure or the credit of a success. These views, he wrote Cobb on February 25, had already been made known to Davis. The following August the Louisiana politician and Mason were accredited to France and England, respectively, Cobb presumably having in the meantime interceded in behalf of Slidell.[1]

On April 12, 1861, the day Fort Sumter fell, Cobb received official word that President Davis had called a special session of Congress to convene in Montgomery on April 29.[2] A few days later he set out for Macon, Georgia, to join his family. On the return trip he stopped in Oxford, Mississippi, to visit friends and make an address in the town's largest church.[3] When he reached Macon about April 20, two of his sons, John A. and Lamar, were already in the military service and preparing to leave for the Virginia front.[4]

With Howell Cobb, Jr. soon to join his older brothers, the elder Cobb realized, as he prepared to return to Montgomery in late April, that his own pattern of life must soon be greatly altered. He had previously confided to his wife that he would retire from politics after the Provisional Congress had completed its work.[5] Public life in the Confederacy had already proved harassing to him. Pressure from office-seekers was particularly heavy. Long before there were offices to fill, requests for patronage began pouring in. Cobb thought half the people of Georgia were in Montgomery, seeking offices, while the other half were at home writing letters on the subject. One applicant

[1] See Frank L. Owsley, *King Cotton Diplomacy* (Chicago, 1931), 70-71.
[2] William M. Browne to Cobb, Apr. 12, 1861.
[3] Mrs. Jacob Thompson to Mrs. Cobb, Apr. 17, 1861.
[4] Lamar Cobb to John A. Cobb, Apr. 19, 1861; *Southern Banner*, May 8, 1861.
[5] See Mrs. Cobb to Cobb, Apr. 3, 1861.

needed an appointment to save him from starvation, another boasted of his prowess at shorthand, and some were even more candid. For example, one preferred a clerkship, "especially one of a pretty good salary," and another inquired, ". . . can I not get a position of profit with some honor attached to it?"[6]

Not only were office-seekers bombarding Cobb with requests for offices before there were any, but Georgia's Governor Joseph E. Brown was challenging the Confederacy before President Davis had been in office a week.[7] The war governor personified the Confederacy's great contradiction. It could be born, but it could not live. Men like Brown and Alexander H. Stephens could readily frame inflammatory metaphors in defense of what they called "liberty," but they seemed never to appreciate the need of balancing that virtue with authority. Unfortunately, the Confederacy produced no statesman who could resolve this contradiction. Cobb, himself, left little convincing evidence that he understood the problem any better than Davis, but the Georgian had certain personal qualities—especially the ability to work with others—that were lacking in Davis. Instinctively, Cobb sided with the President from the start and quickly came to loathe Brown, writing his wife on October 4, after Brown's election to a third term, that with her consent he would take his family out of Georgia and not return "whilst the miserable wretch disgraces the executive chair."

Still other woes were to beset Cobb at the dawn of the Confederacy. Ethusiasm for secession in North Georgia had fallen below expectation. Union sentiment presisted among those who had formerly been his strongest supporters.[8] Almost as distressing was the reluctance of the Upper South to join the youthful nation. Little wonder that Cobb was at times overwhelmed with gloom. An optimist

---

[6] Cobb to John A. Cobb, Feb. 15, Junius Hillyer to Cobb, Feb. 11, Eugene L. Didier to Cobb, Feb. 28, J. W. B. Summers to Cobb, Feb. 18, A. Hood to Cobb, Feb. 5, 1861.

[7] Cobb to his wife, Feb. 23, John A. Cobb to Cobb, Feb. 28, George D. Phillips to Cobb, March 1, 1861.

[8] Jonathan Martin to Cobb, Apr. 15, 1861.

by nature, however, he believed there would be brighter
days. Feeding his optimism was a steady flow of advice
from his Democratic acquaintances in the North. Some of
them had been his subordinates in the Treasury Department. At times they indulged in prophecies which frequently proved faulty. Often they wrote what they mis-
takenly believed would please their Southern friend. Typical
was the correspondence of one who deliberately sought to
raise Cobb's spirits. He claimed to have spoken frequently
and "confidentally" to the boldest Republican leaders. They
did not wish a restoration of the Union, but in the North
there was a strong popular demand for such a course. If
the South would accept it, the Republicans would be succeeded in the government by the Democrats and "then
justice may return."[9]

But Cobb could not adopt such a proposition and still
expect Southern Unionists to join wholeheartedly in the
Confederate cause. Instead, he saw Southern success in
terms of a show of military resistance to the Republicans.
This would drive Southern Unionists into the Confederacy
and Republicans out of Washington, Cobb wrote his wife
on May 3, thus laying a solid basis for negotiation. Cobb
wished to participate directly in this strategy and before
leaving Macon he announced that he would not again seek
public office, but as soon as Congress adjourned he would
go into his old congressional district to raise a regiment
for the Confederate States Army.[10]

The second session of the Confederate Provisional Congress lasted but three weeks. Its president complained that
the delegates were out of touch with developments in the
Federal capital, although this did not prevent him from
prophesying that, unless a conflict occurred within forty
days, there would be no war. This prognostication, he
admitted, was contrary to the "current" of public opinion.[11]
On the other hand, Congress quickly passed a bill re-

[9] J. D. Hoover to Cobb, Apr. 16, 1861.
[10] *Southern Banner*, May 8, 1861; T. R. R. Cobb to his wife, May 3
(Cobb Letters).
[11] Cobb to his wife, May 10, 1861 (Phillips, 565-566).

cognizing the existence of war and, although it never passed a declaration of war, it came close to doing so when on May 6 it sought to remedy the lack of a navy by establishing rules to protect privateering. Later, President Davis resorted to the enlistment of armed ships by offering letters of marque to all who would agree to abide by the rules.[12]

Without a treasury, an army, or a navy, the Congress authorized a bond sale to pay for raising a force of one hundred thousand volunteers. It also enacted legislation which in the opinion of Cobb was designed to take all control of state troops out of the hands of governors. Late in the session Cobb observed that because of this action Governor Brown was "trying to ride the high horse," adding that he would sustain the Confederate authorities, hoping that "the miserable demagogue who now disgraces the executive chair of Georgia" would soon be "thoroughly put down."[13]

While Cobb was in Montgomery, his wife and the younger children returned to Athens. With the adjournment of Congress on May 21 he immediately left to join them. In Atlanta the following day he spoke briefly to a crowd of admirers, explaining that the seat of government was being moved to Richmond for a good reason. Virginia was soon to become the battleground and congressmen, he said, wished to be nearby so they could divide their time and energy between legislating and fighting. He urged his listeners to show their patriotism by buying bonds, praised Southern women, and assured all that the Confederate States of America could not lose their fight for independence because God was on its side.[14]

Cobb was anxious to get his plans for raising a regiment well under way before July 20, the date Congress was to reconvene in Richmond. His stay in Athens was therefore brief, but he was there long enough to discuss with Mrs. Cobb his decision to enter the army. She believed that,

---

[12] James M. Matthews (ed.), *Statutes at Large of the Provisional Government of the Confederate States of America* . . . (Richmond, 1864), 100-104; Coulter, 296.
[13] Cobb to his wife, May 5, 18, 1861 (Phillips, 568).
[14] *Southern Banner*, May 29, 1861.

because he was president of Congress and had three sons in the army, a military career would be unnecessary.[15] In the end, however, she deferred to his wish, as she usually did, and he hurried off to Richmond. On June 14 he wrote her that, although President Davis and the Secretary of War were disposed toward granting him a commission and the authorization to raise a regiment of troops, they had postponed action because of the paucity of arms. He was confident, however, that things would work out as he wished, for already he was being greeted on the streets of Richmond as "Colonel" and "it seems to be well understood that I am shortly to take after the Yankees."

Awaiting a decision from the Confederate authorities, Cobb went off to spend two days with his sons, John A. and Lamar, who were encamped at Sewall Point, north of Norfolk and across Hampton Roads from Fort Monroe. While there, he wrote his wife on June 16, he came under the fire of the Federal "Rip-Raps" at Fort Monroe. Surprised at the coolness of the Confederates, he soon became accustomed to the action and reported that he ate a hearty dinner while the firing continued. He spent the night sleeping on a plank floor with his sons.[16] Thus, as a civilian and in the company of his two sons, Howell Cobb, within three months of his forty-seventh birthday, got his first taste of military life, an experience which unquestionably magnified the importance of what he finally gave as the most compelling reason for his decision to enter the army.

While at Sewall Point Cobb was offered the battalion of four companies—about five hundred men—to which his two sons belonged. The proposal was made by the officers in the hope that their troops would become part of the regiment Cobb was planning to raise. Because he had not yet been authorized to raise a regiment, however, Cobb had to reject the offer. Soon after he returned to Richmond Davis

---

[15] Mrs. Cobb to John B. Lamar, May 30, 1861.
[16] Lamar Cobb to John B. Lamar, June 17, Cobb to his wife, June 20, Lamar to his mother, June 22, 1861.

authorized him to take such action and he immediately
informed the officers at Sewall Point he was now prepared
to accept their offer. He explained to his wife that he had
many reasons for making such an arrangement, the most
compelling being "to be with the boys and to have the four
best drilled companies in the army in my regiment." With
the aid of the experienced officers of this battalion, Cobb
wrote Mrs. Cobb, June 23, that he believed he could quickly
get the remaining six companies of his proposed regiment
ready for combat. However, he failed to get the Sewall
Point troops because the offer was withdrawn.[17] All three
of the Cobbs were disappointed. One of the sons wrote
his uncle that he would apply for a transfer to his father's
command, whatever it was.[18]

Late in June Cobb was back in Georgia to begin the work
of recruiting. Assisting him was Lieutenant James Barrow, recently appointed as his staff adjutant.[19] The War
Department ordered Colonel Cobb to have his regiment
rendezvous in Richmond and warned him to bring along a
good horse and all necessary accoutrements.[20] As he had
so often done, Cobb now turned to John B. Lamar for help,
asking him on June 30 to provide $1000, a sword, and a
colonel's uniform.[21] The two men were very close friends
and over the years they had worked out a satisfactory
arrangement under which Lamar looked after their planting interests while Cobb tended to politics. At this time
Cobb explained to his friend the reasons for his decision
to enter the army. In the first place, he believed it would
have a good effect upon the people of North Georgia. Mindful of their reluctance to accept secession, he confessed to
a major part in getting them to do so and now he felt it

[17] Robert A. Smith to Cobb, June 24, 1861.
[18] John A. Cobb to John B. Lamar, June 27, 1861.
[19] See E. Merton Coulter, *Lost Generation: The Life and Death of
James Barrow, C. S. A.*, Confederate Centennial Studies, No. 1
(Tuscaloosa, 1956).
[20] William M. Browne to Cobb, June 29, 1861.
[21] *Southern Federal Union*, June 25, 1861, reported a uniform con-
sisting of a short tunic of cadet grey and pantaloons of sky-blue had
been adopted. The Cobbs frequently referred to their "blue uniforms."

his duty to take part in a fight he had helped to bring about. But there was a more important reason for his decision, a reason he feared the critics would be unlikely to consider as patriotic: "I had three sons in the army and they were privates. I believed I could provide for and protect them better by being in the army myself. It was to be in a position where I could do this—more certainly and effectively that I have taken this important step."[22]

The work of recruiting ten companies required about six weeks. Because Cobb had to be in Richmond for the opening of Congress on July 20, Lieutenant Barrow was left behind to complete the work. By mid-August all ten companies, totaling approximately nine hundred men, had reached Richmond's Fair Grounds, about one mile from the State House, established Camp Cobb, and had been organized as the Sixteenth Georgia Regiment of Infantry.[23] Cobb arranged to sleep in camp and attend Congress during the day. Until the lawmakers adjourned on August 31 Lieutenant-Colonel Goode Bryan, a competent drill master and veteran of the Mexican War, was actually in charge. Cobb was pleased to have Bryan on his staff, reporting to John B. Lamar, July 28 and August 30, that "he does not drink a drop." Also added to his staff were his two sons, John A. as quartermaster sergeant and Lamar as sergeant major. Reaching the Fair Grounds at about the same time as the Sixteenth Georgia was Cobb's Legion, commanded by Colonel Tom Cobb, which Howell's third son, Howell, Jr., was soon to join, thus bringing to five the number of Georgia Cobbs in the Confederate Army in Virginia.[24]

On July 21, the day after Congress convened, the United States Army was summarily defeated at the First Battle of Manassas. The elder Cobbs shared the optimism that now swept Richmond. Shortly after the engagement Tom Cobb wrote Howell that it was one of the world's decisive

[22] Cobb to John B. Lamar, June 30, 1861.
[23] John A. Cobb to John B. Lamar, Aug. 17, 1861; Coulter, *Lost Generation*, 58.
[24] John A. Cobb to John B. Lamar, Aug. 28, 1861; *Southern Banner*, Nov. 6, 1861.

battles, because it "has secured our Independence."[25] The latter was equally sanguine. He thought the Federal government would now wage war with "fury and malignity" and "we will have to whip them again & badly." What encouraged him most were the reports that there was already much peace talk in the North, that volunteering had fallen off, and that before the first of the year Yankee finances would be in a state of collapse. He did not doubt that England and France would soon recognize the Confederacy and quickly end the blockade. He assured both his wife and his brother-in-law, John B. Lamar, that peace would come in but four or five months.[26]

With the adjournment of Congress on August 31, Cobb assumed personal charge of his regiment. Within ten days he received orders to move it to Yorktown to join the already victorious army of General John B. Magruder, whose task was to prevent the Federal forces at Fort Monroe from moving up the Peninsula toward Richmond.[27] However, because of sickness and the lack of arms, Cobb was unable to move his regiment for five weeks. During early September many of the men were stricken with mumps and measles.[28] One of the company commanders attributed these epidemics to the prevalance of country boys, explaining that because of their rural backgrounds they had previously escaped such diseases.[29] On September 7 Cobb reported seven deaths. Two weeks later the number had doubled. John A. Cobb wrote John B. Lamar on September 22 that several deaths had been caused by the carelessness of convalescents. He reported one soldier as taking "a bath under a pump while the fever was on him. . . ." Cobb tried to remedy such behavior by enforcing stricter dis-

[25] July 24, 1861 (Cobb Letters).
[26] Cobb to John B. Lamar, July 28, 30, 1861; Cobb to his wife, Aug. 6, 1861 (Phillips, 573).
[27] Magruder had defeated the enemy at Big Bethel, June 10, the first battle of the war. See John A. Cobb to John B. Lamar, Sept. 12, 1861; Douglas Southall Freeman, *Lee's Lieutenants* . . . (New York, 1942), I, 17-18.
[28] John A. Cobb to John B. Lamar, Sept. 8, 1861.
[29] *Southern Banner*, Oct. 16, 1861. See also Bell I. Wiley, *Life of Johnny Reb* . . . (Indianapolis, 1942), 246.

cipline, admitting he had to fill the guard tent more than
once for disobedience.   He boasted that he had the cleanest
and neatest camp in the service and predicted that he would
have few disciplinary problems in the future.   Harsh discipline was softened with a show of sympathy for the sick.
"I visit them daily," Cobb wrote his wife "to cheer them
up and often with a bleeding heart I smooth their foreheads
with my hand. . . ."[30]
As the number of deaths increased, ugly rumors began
to circulate back home, according to Mrs. Cobb.   On
September 13 she wrote that rumor had it that the death
rate in the Sixteenth Georgia was six men per day.   Another alleged that Cobb had had one of his company commanders flogged because he moved his sick out of camp.[31]
When the Augusta *Constitutionalist* published these rumors,
Mrs. Cobb wrote James Gardner, Jr., the editor, a letter
signed "Truth" in which she denied the story about the
number of deaths in her husband's regiment.   She offered
Cobb a lengthy defense of her action, claiming that "there
was a *spirit*—(not 'pale ale') (Old Bourbon nor Old Rye)—
but a controlling spirit that urged me on and dictated to
me."[32]
On October 4 Cobb reported to his wife that his regiment
was mustering almost its entire strength.   In five weeks
slightly under thirty men had died.   Some Georgia regiments were said to have lost as many as one hundred men,
but on October 6 Cobb complained to John B. Lamar that
nothing had been written in the Georgia press about them.
To his wife he explained the cause of his unfavorable
publicity.   He had attempted to keep his sick in camp
when some had wished to go to private homes and hospitals
in town.   A few had left camp without permission and had
gone about, seeking quarters.   This had given rise to
rumors "which a few meddling women have amused themselves in adding to and circulating. . . ."   He requested

[30] Cobb to his wife, Sept. 7, 8, 22, 1861.
[31] J. D. Frierson to Cobb, Oct. 4, 1861.
[32] Mrs. Cobb to Cobb, Sept. 13, 19, 1861.

her to have James Jackson write an editorial for the Athens *Southern Banner* to squelch the rumors by presenting the facts. This editorial seems never to have been written, but throughout the period of the epidemics and for weeks thereafter numerous reassuring pieces did appear in this paper.[33]

Arming the Sixteenth Georgia Regiment turned into an experience about as disconcerting as any Colonel Cobb was to have while at Camp Cobb. Around the middle of September he sent a special agent to Savannah to bring back a shipment of Enfield rifles that had been brought through the blockade. A short time later he went to Richmond to receive the arms, only to learn they had been seized by Governor Brown. He lost his usual self-control and demanded of the authorities that such interference cease. His outburst produced a wire to Savannah and a reply that all but 1,000 of the guns would be released promptly. Following the incident, on September 30 Cobb wrote his wife: "I feel like a piece of timber floating on the current, with no power to control my course or destiny."

When the Enfields finally reached Richmond in mid-October, they were found to be rusty. Another four or five days delay in arming the regiment resulted. Nonetheless, Cobb finally got the weapons and his friend William M. Browne, now an important official in the Confederate State Department, congratulated him on having the best guns in the Confederate Army. He also let Cobb know in a letter dated October 23 that he had worked hard to bring about the happy result. "Let us know," he concluded, "if the 16th Ga. Regt. wants socks, clothes or comforts. I can control supplies & send them if needed."[34]

When he was not looking after the sick or trying to get guns, Cobb was busy learning the routine duties of a military commander. On October 14, John Cobb wrote his mother, the Colonel was far enough along to shout drill orders from horseback.

[33] See *Southern Banner*, Oct. 23, Nov. 6, Dec. 11, 1861, and Jan. 15, 1862; Cobb to Mrs. Cobb, Nov. 18, 1861.
[34] See also Briscoe G. Baldwin to Cobb, Oct. 14, 1861.

A few days later the Sixteenth's morale was boosted by the fact that on August 28 Congress had approved Cobb's colonelcy and the following day unanimously resolved that President Davis present him a "stand of colors and a sword" as a testimonial of the high esteem in which he was held by its members. Cobb responded to the latter with a "pretty little speech."[35] On September 21 the President wrote the Colonel that the stand of colors would be presented by his aide-de-camp . . . "and you will accept assurance of the confidence I feel that this flag, intrusted to you . . . will be gallantly borne wherever our country's need may claim it."[36] The presentation did not take place until October 17, a day of threatening clouds and rain. On hand for the occasion were Colonel Cobb and his staff, the President's brother, Joseph Davis, who represented him, other high Confederate officials, a military band which played "Dixie," and a large crowd of civilians. Upon receipt of the banner, Cobb responded by saying that he entrusted it to the hands of his men, that if ever the regiment encountered the enemy it must become the rallying cry, "and rather than surrender it, let it wave over the burial-ground of every man in the regiment."[37]

At last Cobb was ready to carry out his orders to move down the Peninsula to join General Magruder. His men were now in good health and well armed and they had been ceremoniously exhorted by their commander to fight and, if necessary, die for the Confederacy. To bring his regiment to this state of readiness, Cobb had endured some experiences that were hardly calculated to inspire his patriotism. What disturbed him most was the biting criticism of those who, like himself, were alleged to have been awarded commissions because they had been prominent public figures. They were sometimes facetiously called

[35] *Journal of the Congress*, I, 435, 440, 441; T. R. R. Cobb to his wife, Aug. 30, 1861 (Cobb Letters).
[36] *War of the Rebellion* . . . (Washington, 1880-1901), 4 Series, I, 615 (hereinafter cited as *ORA*).
[37] *Southern Banner*, Oct. 23, Nov. 6, 1861; Coulter, *Lost Generation*, 61.

"Warrior Statesmen."[38] Their critics were often the spokes-
men of the "West Point crowd," whose depth of feeling is
well illustrated by the private correspondence of Colonel
LaFayette McLaws, a native Georgian who had been gradu-
ated from West Point in 1842 and had served in the Mexican War. Upon hearing that the Cobb brothers had been
ordered to the Peninsula, McLaws wrote his wife, September 29, "I am getting much disposed to come home. The
Cobbs are coming over to the Peninsula. . . . And report
says Howell will come as a Brigadier General. I do not
wish to be under any politician, nor will I if it can be
helped."[39]

Although President Davis was accused of siding with
the "West Point crowd" and of treating Cobb shabbily, the
latter never engaged either openly or secretly in such
machinations as were ascribed to Brigadier-General Robert
Toombs.[40] Of Toombs it was confidentially reported by
William M. Browne to Cobb on November 4, 1861 that he
"is doing all he can to fan the flames to devour J[efferson]
D[avis] and that it is a concerted scheme in the interest
of A. H. S[tephe]ns." To be sure, Cobb believed Davis
obstinate and privately accused him of seeing no good outside West Point in military matters. He wrote his wife on
January 25, 1862 that the President had carried his bias
to the extent of preferring "drunken West Point men . . .
to worthy and accomplished men from private life. . . ."

On the morning of October 19, 1861 the Sixteenth Georgia
Regiment broke camp, boarded the cars of the Richmond
and York River Rail Road for West Point, from whence
it embarked on the steamer C. S. S. *Logan* for Yorktown.
The trip downstream was a welcome diversion. There was
music by a brass band. The men shot their rifles at birds
and otherwise relaxed.[41] Reaching Yorktown at nightfall,
the regiment marched half a mile to a grove of scrubby

[38] *Southern Banner*, Sept. 4, 1861.
[39] McLaws Papers (in University of North Carolina Library,
Chapel Hill).
[40] T. R. R. Cobb to his wife, Jan. 27, 1862 (Cobb Letters).
[41] *Southern Banner*, Nov. 6, 1861.

cedars along the river bank, where the men slept on the
wet ground. The next morning they marched to Camp
Bryan, near Grafton Church, which was about three miles
south of Yorktown on the road to Newport News. The
new camp was a clover field surrounded by a forest of ripe
chestnuts, chinquepins, grapes, and walnuts. Wild turkeys
were plentiful and oysters were in abundance. The early
days were happy ones, the men enjoying especially the
novelty of cracking oysters.[42]

The Sixteenth Georgia Regiment was now a part of
General John B. Magruder's "Army of the Peninsula," a
unit of less than ten thousand men whose duty it was to
protect the area from possible attack by Federals at Fort
Monroe. Colonel Cobb was in frequent conference with
"Prince John," as Magruder was called, and quickly developed a fondness for him. Both Cobb and his brother
Tom, whose Georgia Legion was now encamped a few miles
south of Camp Bryan, believed Magruder a competent,
though somewhat excitable, officer who was being unfairly
charged with a weakness for strong drink.[43]

Cobb quickly settled down to the severe routine of Camp
Bryan. Often he spent the entire day and part of the night
in the saddle, supervising the construction of fortifications.
On October 29 he wrote his wife that he had come to "feel
more like an 'Irish ditcher' than the Col. of a Ga. Regiment."
Interminable rains did not help construction efforts, but
worse on morale was the psychological impact of grim
tents huddled above the surface of a squashy flat marsh,
recently a clover field, where soldiers with guns and knap-
sacks sloshed about to give a touch of weirdness outside
the ken of most of the inhabitants of Camp Bryan.[44]

Into this clammy fall atmosphere came an unwelcome
visitor, a parisitic mite that bred and burrowed in the skin

[42] John A. Cobb to John B. Lamar, Oct. 21, 1861.
[43] Lamar Cobb to John B. Lamar, Oct. 23, 1861; Cobb to R. M. T.
Hunter, Oct. 21, 1861 (*ORA*, 1 Series, IV, 865) ; T. R. R. Cobb to his
wife, Jan. 9, 1862 (Cobb Letters) ; Freeman, I, 160.
[44] Cobb to his wife, Nov 13, John A. Cobb to John B. Lamar, Oct.
27, 29, 1861.

of the soldiers, creating an abiding desire to scratch. Cobb
had already had his fill of camp sickness and this outbreak
of the itch further enraged him. He isolated the victims
and on November 1 wrote his wife that "when they are
all well—we shall burn the tent and have the dirty devils
regularly washed."

To make matters worse there developed friction between
soldiers and civilians. Cobb's Georgians were not exactly
fond of Virginians. One of his sons thought they were the
meanest people he had ever been among, and Colonel Tom
Cobb described them as a "selfish, grasping, unpatriotic
set of treacherous rascals."[45] More annoying than Virginians, and especially to the normally sanguine Cobb, was
the persistence of the enemy; "but they must fall," he wrote
his wife on November 8, "before the strong arm of right and
justice and sooner or later we shall have peace and independence."

As is frequently the habit of the soldier, Cobb sought
relief from his frustrations by acquiring "camp talk,"
growing a beard, and taking in the local sights. He allowed
some of his newly-acquired expletives to slip into letters to
his wife, for which on October 27 she mildly admonished
him in these words: "I must say, if that language you used
is a specimen of 'camp talk'—I fear you and my boys will
return rather worsted than improved. If you must use
such—I will get Mary Ann [Cobb's oldest daughter] to
look up the French for such . . . so as to give your conversation & writing a shade of elegance & refinement."
As for shaving, it was probably during these monotonous
days that he quit the custom. At any rate, he appeared in
Athens late in November, 1861 with a luxuriant mustache
and beard. One observer was satisfied that it was a disguise designed to protect him in battle. Another thought it
had made him "ugly enough to frighten the devil."[46]

Cobb was aware of the rich history of the Virginia

[45] John A. Cobb to John B. Lamar, and to his mother, Oct. [n. d.],
Dec. 1, 1861; T. R. R. Cobb to his wife, Sept. 24, 1861 (Cobb Letters).
[46] Mrs. Cobb to John B. Lamar, Dec. 6, 1861.

Peninsula. Near his headquarters General Washington had received the surrender of Lord Cornwallis. To learn more of the military operations that had occurred here during the Revolution, Cobb requested a copy of Lossing's *Pictorial Field Book of the Revolution*. Of more immediate personal interest to the Colonel and his brother was the home of their maternal ancestors at "White Marsh," eight miles from Yorktown, which they vistied in early November. Here they observed a magnificient house and expansive gardens, situated on a high bluff overlooking an estate of 2,000 acres of flat land. They viewed their grandfather Rootes' grave and were surprised to learn he had died before he was sixty years old. An elderly inhabitant invited them to dinner and ventured the opinion that Howell reminded him of grandfather Rootes.[47]

Despite such morale-boosting improvisations, Cobb, now forty-six years old and unaccustomed to the hardships of military life, was beset with gloom. "I find," he wrote his wife on November 1, after less than two weeks on the Peninsula, "that it taxes all my time and energy to attend to one regiment." And then in an unusual mood of self-pity he added that he could expect little help from the Davis administration because he was not among its favorites. A few days later the Cobb brothers addressed a joint letter to the War Department, requesting transfer of their commands to Georgia.[48] Upon hearing this, Mrs. Cobb facetiously inquired on November 29 whether Howell wished to serve under Governor Brown. He was spared this discomfiture, because the request went unheeded.

With the final session of the Provisional Congress scheduled to convene on November 18, Cobb planned to alternate between Richmond and the command of the Sixteenth Georgia. Although Magruder daily expected a fight near Yorktown, Cobb had strong feelings to the contrary and proceeded with arrangements to attend the opening

[47] Mrs. Cobb to Cobb, Nov. 3, 1861; Cobb to his wife, Nov. 8, 1861 (Cobb Folder).
[48] T. R. R. Cobb to his wife, Nov. 5, 1861 (Cobb Letters).

of Congress.[49] Before he left he considered resigning his office as president of the Congress, but explained that, if he were to take this step, he would retain his membership in that body "for the benefit of the army whose claims & wants are only known to those who have to experience them."

Cobb reached Richmond in the midst of the excitement caused by the news of the arrest on November 8 of Mason and Slidell, the Confederate envoys to England and France, respectively. Their seizure from the *Trent*, a British merchantman, by the captain of the U. S. S. *San Jacinto* constituted in Cobb's opinion a violation of international rights. The course England would pursue was now the big question. Like many others, Cobb believed the fate of the Confederacy depended on England's action. About all the authorities in Richmond could do, however, was to await developments between London and Washington. Cobb predicted that President Davis would delay his message to Congress until he could make a positive reference to England's disposition of the matter.[50] It is possible that Cobb, once invited by Presidents Pierce and Buchanan to confer on important matters of state, expected a similar offer from Davis. However, no such overture was forthcoming, nor did the President delay his message. Indeed, his only reference to the *Trent* affair was an accusation of the Lincoln government for having wantonly violated British rights.[51]

There was much jubilation in Richmond over the *Trent* affair. England's war preparations encouraged the belief that at last that country was making ready to enter the American conflict on the side of the Confederacy. The blockade, which John B. Lamar believed would become serious in another year, would thus be broken. When the

[49] Cobb to Alexander H. Stephens, Nov. 2, 5, 1861 (in Stephens Papers, Emory University Library, Atlanta, Ga.) ; Cobb to his wife, Nov. 8, 1861 (Cobb Folder).
[50] Cobb to John B. Lamar, Nov. 14, and to his wife, Nov. 18, 1861.
[51] James D. Richardson (comp.), *A Compilation of the Messages and Papers of the Confederacy* (Nashville, 1905), I, 141-142.

United States made proper apologies and the prospect of intervention vanished, Secretary of the Treasury C. G. Memminger wrote Cobb: "I am sorry for this as I confidently hoped for a speedy end to the Blockade. I still hope almost against hope for some further complication between them and England."[52] Despite this set-back to the Confederate cause, Cobb clung for months to the slender hope that John Bull would yet go after the "cowardly Yankee Govt. . . . God speed him in all he does to destroy Yankeedom."[53]

At the height of the jubilation over the *Trent* affair Cobb left Richmond for a short visit with his family. He was back in Richmond in early December to find "Congress busily engaged in *talking*." He "caught the mania . . . ," writing his wife on December 5 that he had already made a speech giving "one black eye" to a recommendation of Secretary of War Judah P. Benjamin and thought he might "put the other one out tomorrow."

In charge of the Sixteenth Georgia Regiment during Cobb's absence was Lieutenant-Colonel Goode Bryan, who in December had begun preparations for the construction of a winter camp.[54] Progress was slow. There were logs to be hauled and not enough wagons to do the job. The sawmill was shut down, because the sawyer had left camp to procure a casting. If Cobb located him in Richmond, he was urged by Bryan (December 4, 1861) "to tie him, kick him and send him back home." The weather was biting cold, snow flurries were frequent, and the wind was strong "enough to blow the horns off the head of a Billy goat." Bryan's troubles were multiplied by the arrival of a new sutler, who broke Cobb's orders by selling liquor the first evening. "I sent him a three corner this morning," Bryan reported to his commander, "and informed the gentleman

---

[52] Jan. 1, 1862 (Phillips, 587); see also John B. Lamar to Cobb, Nov. 3, 1861.

[53] Cobb to his wife, Nov. 18, Dec. 5, 1861, Jan. 6, 18, 1862; *Southern Banner*, Nov. 27, 1861.

[54] John A. Cobb to his mother, Dec. 1, 1861.

that if he sold any more I would close him up and send him off. I was cross with him. . . ."

Over and above these and other internal woes was the excitement caused by reports that the enemy might attack at any moment. Such reports were repeatedly issued by General Magruder, who persisted in taking counsel of his fears. In mid-December he cancelled all furloughs and ordered Cobb, two days after the Colonel had concluded a week's duty with his regiment, to return to the Peninsula at once.[55] Mrs. Cobb wrote her husband that the order cancelling the furloughs came as a shocking surprise to many Georgians. Some even questioned Magruder's sobriety, she declared. With difficulty she defended the "Old Hero of Bethel," disclosing that already many had begun to snicker at the frequent reports in the letters of Cobb's sons "that Pa is with Genl. Magruder." On December 22 she assured her husband she was not uneasy about him, "but if I continue to defend your General you *must watch* over him."

A few days before Christmas Cobb returned to the Sixteenth. It had recently moved to the unfinished winter quarters on the Yorktown-Williamsburg Road, less than two miles from Yorktown. Named in honor of Mrs. Cobb's brother, Camp Lamar was on the very ground occupied by Washington's army before the surrender of Cornwallis. Cobb was to remain with his regiment until after the middle of January, supervising the completion of Camp Lamar, responding to alarms, and improving discipline among the troops.[56]

Camp Lamar was finally finished on January 10. By that time all the men were living in log cabins. Cobb's was a double cabin, each unit measuring 16 x 18 ft., with a 10 ft. connecting passage. He was pleased with his new quarters and its rough furniture, which included a bedstead whose bottom was a plank. Next to the plank he spread a buffalo

[55] John A. Cobb to his mother, Dec. 16, 1861.
[56] *Southern Banner*, Jan. 15, 1862; Cobb to his wife, Dec. 22, 1861 (Cobb Folder) ; Coulter, *Lost Generation*, 65.

robe and one blanket. Softer beds he had seen, but he assured his wife that "no beds have ever seen harder sleepers." Nightly alarms, constant marching to positions, and waiting in rain and sleet for Yankees, who, according to Cobb, had no notion of "coming this way at this time," became operational procedure. The increased tempo was induced by the gathering of a Federal amphibious force in the Chesapeake Bay. Commanded by Commodore Louis M. Goldsborough, with General Ambrose E. Burnside in charge of the ground troops, its destination was for a time unknown to the Confederates. Until it slipped out of Hampton Roads on January 11, the excitable Magruder kept Cobb in the saddle until he tired of what he called "this amusement." The Georgian protested that he would be "agreeably disappointed," if after the vigil he escaped without a few corns on his hips and thighs.

Throughout the early weeks at Camp Lamar Cobb retained his sense of humor and his affection for "Prince John" Magruder, whom he described as "a wise, prudent and able general" and under whom he would as soon serve "as any officer in the field."[57] He even defended the alarms, "for without them our soldiers would forget that it was war—and that would unfit them for their work."[58] He was genuinely concerned about the Georgia recruits who had volunteered for twelve months with the Confederate Army in Virginia. Many were known to have no desire to re-enlist; besides, they wanted to take their arms home with them. If this happened, Cobb wrote his wife on January 18, 1862, the Confederacy would stand to lose both men and arms. He was also disturbed by those young men who were "dodging" the army by joining state units in the hope of easier duty.[59] Convinced that the professional attitude toward the civilian soldier discouraged volunteering, he wrote Secretary of the Treasury Memminger, urging that President Davis request all generals

[57] Cobb to his wife, Jan. 1, 6, 10, 1862.
[58] Cobb to Meyon [Mary Ann, his daughter] Jan. 13, 1862.
[59] John A. Cobb to his father, Feb. 15, 1862.

to temper discipline with kindness. Memminger replied that Davis had promised to do all he could to tone down the "old habits" of the high-ranking officers and concluded by expressing the hope that Cobb himself would soon "be up here to assist the necessary legislation to carry out these plans."[60]

So it was—when Howell Cobb was in Richmond, he received urgent requests from General Magruder and Lieutenant-Colonel Bryan to return to Yorktown; when he was in Yorktown, political leaders wanted him back in Richmond. Late in 1861 some Virginians even asked him to come to the Capital City to support Secretary of State R. M. T. Hunter's candidacy for a seat in the Senate. Cobb had already written a letter which was published in the Richmond *Enquirer*, urging Hunter's election. However, some of Hunter's friends in the Virginia legislature believed he would bring the state greater honor by remaining where he was. Cobb was expected to meet with these legislators in Richmond's Exchange Hotel early in 1862 and acquaint them "with the points of power in the govt." Whether he ever met them is uncertain but, when the permanent Confederate government began operating on February 22, Hunter was one of Virginia's senators.[61]

Inclement weather, construction problems, alarms, and the demands of politics were not the only troubles confronting Cobb and the men of the Sixteenth Georgia. Newspapers were few and letters from home were often in transit for as long as three weeks.[62] One of Cobb's sons thought the trouble with the mails could be traced to Petersburg. From that station to Richmond, he stated, the railroad was "*owned* most at the *North* and it is the most unaccomidating [sic] there is in the Confederate States."[63]

Despite the vicissitudes of his double life, Cobb could

[60] Jan. 1, 1862 (Phillips, 587).
[61] L. Q. Washington to Cobb, Dec. 31, 1861; Henry H. Simms, *Life of Robert M. T. Hunter* . . . (Richmond, 1935), 193.
[62] Cobb to his wife, Jan. 6, to Meyon, Jan. 13, 1862.
[63] John A. Cobb to John B. Lamar, Jan. 1, 1862.

take satisfaction from a number of solid accomplishments.
By the time he was ready to return to Richmond in mid-
January, 1862, Camp Lamar had been completed. In consequence, his men were now comfortably housed and their
health was reported as good.[64] Unlike Camp Cobb, the
new camp was equipped with hospitals which had been
provided by the conversion of numerous local tobacco
factories. Dr. James Mercer Green was in charge. Thus,
there was no longer the danger of a repetition of the
frightening epidemics of mumps and measles which the men
of the Sixteenth had suffered in old Camp Cobb.[65]

When Cobb reached Richmond, the Confederate Provisional Congress was entering the last five weeks of its
existence. As it turned out, this meant his political career,
reaching back a quarter century, was rapidly drawing to
a close. His private correspondence as well as his public
acts reflected for the first time a deep concern for the Confederacy's future. Formerly, it will be recalled, he had
persisted in the belief that peace was months, perhaps only
weeks, from realization. Now he was certain a crisis was
approaching. Under General George B. McClellan the enemy
was preparing a mighty offensive. The Confederacy was to
be surrounded and dealt what he feared might well be a
crushing blow. This plan, which he learned from the New
York *Evening Post,* looked formidable to Cobb. It became
doubly impressive in the face of the widespread belief that
the twelve-months' men were not anxious to re-enlist. Cobb
came very close to succumbing to defeatism.

Adding to Cobb's anxiety was the feeling in Congress
toward President Davis. "I might almost use the term
odious," he wrote his wife on January 25, 1862, describing
this feeling. Only the condition of the country prevented
an open and unrelenting war upon Davis and "it looks
strange but it is true—that I—(who have never received
a kindness at his hands)—have to interpose between him
and his former pets to save him from bitter attacks on

[64] *Southern Banner,* Jan. 15, 1862.
[65] James Mercer Green to John B. Lamar, Dec. 16, 1861.

the floor of Congress." Cobb explained that he wished no thanks from the President, "for it is no personal kindness or regard for him that prompts me." The country's welfare, he insisted, must be placed before all personal considerations. "Davis is preverse and obstinate," he continued, "and unless we can beat some liberal and just notions into his head—we shall have much trouble in the future—which could easily be avoided."

It is not strange that Cobb's instinctive optimism gave way to a frightening desperation during the early months of the new year. When the rumor reached Richmond in mid-January that one of the objectives of the Burnside-Goldsborough invasion was to be Savannah, he privately advocated for the first time a "scorched earth" policy. A few days later he repeated, again privately, that the South must be aroused and make "manifest to the North that any alternative is preferable to association with them. The burning of cotton and houses and property . . . was worth a great battle. Let the North see in the hand of every Southern man, woman & child a torch ready to be applied to their dwellings & property rather than to see it fall into the hands of the vandal robbers & we shall soon have peace and independence."[66]

Early in February he joined his brother, Brigadier-General Toombs, and M. J. Crawford in an "Address to the People of Georgia" in which the citizens were reminded that the enemy "comes with lust in his eye, poverty in his purse, and hell in his heart." He must be greeted with fire. Georgians were exhorted to "let every woman have a torch, every child a fireband—let the loved homes of youth be made ashes, and the fields of our heritage be made desolate."[67]

Soon after the completion of the address, Cobb left for Macon, where his family was spending the winter. He was there only a few days, returning north by way of Savan-

[66] Cobb to his wife, Jan. 18, 23, 1862.
[67] *Southern Federal Union*, Feb. 11, 1862; Frank Moore (ed.), *Rebellion Record* . . . (New York, 1861-1868), IV, 192-193.

nah and Charleston. In Savannah he conferred with General Henry Rootes Jackson, a cousin, to whom had been entrusted that city's defense. The two agreed that the Georgia seaport must be burned rather than turned over to the enemy. "If Savannah falls" he wrote his wife, ". . . let it be to the enemy a dearly bought victory and one of ashes." Within a year Cobb, once a renowned conciliator, had become a bitter advocate of force and destruction. Such was the price of war.

Happily, Cobb's recommendations were not adopted. However, two Confederate reverses in February convinced him entirely of the wisdom of putting the torch to homes and fields. On February 8 Roanoke Island fell to Burnside; a week later came the disaster at Fort Donelson. Because of the "cowardly and disgraceful" behavior of Confederate troops, Cobb thought the former a really serious blow.[68]

There was little cause for jubilation as Colonel Howell Cobb, president of the Provisional Congress of the Confederate States of America, arose on February 17 to deliver his valedictory. He reminded his colleagues that on February 22, Washington's birthday, the new permanent government was to be appropriately inaugurated. On that day in the enemy Capitol there would be a "cold, heartless, and hypocritical" ceremony, the annual reading of Washington's Farewell Address. By constantly disregarding the great legacy, the North had forced the South to seek "safety and security in a new organization." He denied the enemy's charge that the new Confederacy was a military despotism. True, in the beginning the Provisional Congress had had almost unlimited power, but it had drafted a charter and was now preparing to surrender to the successor provided by that document. By their action the members had wrought a revolution to escape from "anarchy" and to preserve the "conservative principles" of the Founding Fathers. They had done this without the

[68] Cobb to his wife, Feb. 13, 18, 1862.

benefit of that recognition which had never before been denied a people who had shown the same capacity and determination to maintain independence. The past year, he continued, had demonstrated the accuracy of his prediction that separation was "perfect, complete, and perpetual." After assuring his listeners that he had not experienced "one despondent hour," he discharged the last duty of the chair by pronouncing the Congress adjourned.

On February 22 Howell Cobb called into session the House of Representatives of the newly reorganized Congress of the Confederate States of America and administered the oath to its speaker, Thomas S. Bocock of Virginia. Thus did he simultaneously relinquish his post in the government and cut short his own political career. Only a soldier now, he was never again to return to public life.[69]

[69] *Journal of the Congress*, I, 845-846; V, 5-7.

Chapter III

The Peninsular Campaign

WHEN HOWELL COBB was finally relieved of his onerous civilian responsibilities, he was no longer a colonel. Ten days earlier the Provisional Congress had approved the President's recommendation that he be promoted to the rank of brigadier-general.[1] With his new status came a brighter outlook. Early in March, 1862 he observed that the public was fast recovering from the panic induced by the recent military reverses; indeed, he saw a return of the old spirit of defiance and resistance. In his opinion the new government deserved much credit for the changing mood. However, he reported that President Davis was still far from being popular. Few had confidence either in him or his Cabinet. Cobb himself was greatly encouraged by the rumor that a commanding general was to be placed in charge of the army. "General Lee," he wrote his wife, "will be the man and I think will make a good officer."[2] His prediction was unique, coming at a time when few men appreciated Lee's great powers of leadership. It may have suggested, on Cobb's part, an above-average insight into the recognition of military talent.

Cobb was confident that, while much hard work lay ahead, the Confederacy would yet thwart Yankee plans. These he described as aimed at the separation of Kentucky, Tennessee, Virginia, and North Carolina from the cotton states. Once these four states were subjugated, the Union

[1] *Ibid.*, I, 811.
[2] March 4, 20, 1862. See also Cobb to John B. Lamar, March 7, 1862.

would attempt to crush the remainder of the Confederacy. In order to seize Virginia and North Carolina, the enemy must first take Norfolk and Suffolk. With these cities in his possession, he would then besiege the two important railroads extending southward, one connecting Suffolk with Petersburg, the other with Weldon, North Carolina. Cobb believed the Burnside-Goldsborough expedition, which had already captured New Bern, Morehead City, and other North Carolina towns, was aiming at Weldon.

The retention of Suffolk thus became during the winter of 1861-1862 an important part of the Confederate defense plan. Accordingly, two of General Magruder's brigades were ordered to that strategic city. The first to arrive was that of Brigadier-General George W. Randolph. The other was Cobb's newly-formed Second Brigade, which was conposed of the Sixteenth Georgia Regiment (Cobb's original command), the Georgia Legion (Tom Cobb's unit), the Twenty-fourth Georgia Regiment, the Fifteenth North Carolina Regiment, and the Second Louisiana Regiment. Numbering more than five thousand men, it was probably the largest of Magruder's brigades. On March 7 it arrived at Suffolk; the next day Cobb assumed command. He was immediately placed under Major-General W. W. Loring, the commandant at Suffolk.[3]

Cobb at once began a study of the terrain in the vicinity of Suffolk, selecting positions in preparation for a possible attack.[4] However, in less than two weeks he was ordered to move his brigade to Goldsboro, North Carolina, about one hundred and twenty miles southwest of Suffolk, and about sixty miles inland from New Bern. The journey to the North Carolina city was made on the Wilmington and Weldon Rail Road.[5] Arriving on March 22, the brigade chose a camp site a few miles outside the city and named it Camp Randolph in honor of George W. Randolph, who had

[3] Cobb to John B. Lamar, Feb. 22 (Phillips, 588-589), March 17, 1862. See Freeman, I, 204.
[4] Cobb to his wife, March 20, 1862.
[5] *ORA*, 1 Series, IX, 449. The order was dated March 20, 1862.

just been appointed Secretary of War.[6] Within a week Cobb
reported about twenty thousand men were being concentrated
at Goldsboro under Major-General T. H. Holmes to drive the
enemy from the Tar Heel state.   The arrival of Cobb's
brigade brought the number to well over half the total.

Because Goldsboro was a little nearer home, Cobb's men
soon forgot many of their inconveniences.   However, their
recent movements from the Peninsula to Suffolk and thence
to Goldsboro had kept them well ahead of their wagons and
much-needed equipment and supplies were thus frequently
inadequate.   To make matters worse, at Camp Randolph
there was sickness, especially among the men of the Sixteenth and Twenty-Fourth regiments.   Cobb's staff, which
was literally created on the run, was not entitled to either
a surgeon or a chaplain, its commander good-naturedly observing that the "army makes no provision for the pre-
servation of a General & his staff either in this world or the
world to come."   By late March he and his staff were
satisfactorily housed, however, and his regimental commanders were busy drilling their men for a review in honor
of Major-General Holmes.[7]

In April Cobb's brigade was ordered to rejoin Magruder's
army of the Peninsula, at Yorktown, which was being
threatened by the landing at Fort Monroe of the Army of
the Potomac under General George B. McClellan.[8]   The
Union commander planned to move up the Peninsula and
seize Richmond. Magruder proposed to stop him by station-
ing his army, which on April 12 became part of General
Joseph E. Johnston's command, southward from Yorktown
toward the James River on the western side of the Warwick River, a small stream rising a short distance from
Yorktown and flowing southward across the Peninsula to
the James River.   On the upper reaches of the Warwick
were two dams that had been built before the war.   One of

[6] Coulter, *Lost Generation*, 68.
[7] Cobb to his wife, March 20, 29, Mrs. Cobb to Cobb, March 27, W. L.
Sumter to John A. Cobb, April 5, John A. Cobb to his mother, April 1,
1862.
[8] *ORA*, 1 Series, XI, pt. 3, 425.

them, known as Dam No. 2, was near Wynn's Mill; the
other, about three miles farther south at Lee's Mill, was
known as Dam No. 1.[9] Between the two, Magruder's en-
gineers had hastily constructed others. Below Dam No. 1
the Warwick was too wide for the construction of dams.
Above this point the dams served to impede the enemy by
inundating the low-lying country.[10]

In mid-April Cobb wrote his wife from Magruder's headquarters that the Union and Confederate armies were
drawn up on opposite sides of the Warwick River, within
a half mile of each other. He estimated the Confederate
force at about forty thousand men, with reinforcements
arriving daily.[11] His own brigade, now assigned to Brigadier-General McLaws' Second Division, on April 4 had
taken its position in the Yorktown-Warwick line on a
section adjacent to Lee's Mill. The men were without tents
and, except for trees, had no covering to protect them from
the almost incessant rain that was filling the trenches in
which they lived. John A. Cobb expressed the opinion that
the move back to the Peninsula had not been popular,
although the elder Cobb described the morale of his men
as good and boasted on April 15 that the Georgians alone
were sufficiently numerous to whip the Yankees.[12]

From the time of the arrival on the Yorktown-Warwick
line until mid-April Cobb's brigade, as did its companion
units, simply waited. Offensive action was impossible,
because of inundations from the Warwick River.[13] Nor
were the Yankees active, except for reconnaissance parties
probing for information about Confederate strength and
dispositions. In consequence, a kind of "Sitzkrieg" ensued,
with opposing soldiers engaging each other in amusing and
exaggerated verbal exchanges.[14]

[9] Coulter, *Lost Generation*, 70.
[10] Freeman, I, 148.
[11] April 15, 1862 (Phillips, 594).
[12] *Official Reports of Battles* (Richmond, 1862), 501-508; John A.
Cobb to John B. Lamar, April 6, 1862.
[13] Freeman, I, 148.
[14] T. R. R. Cobb to his wife, April 10, 1862 (Cobb Letters).

On April 16 Cobb's brigade was given its first serious test. Early in the morning two pieces of Union artillery began pounding the Confederate center near Lee's Mill (Dam No. 1). They kept up a steady fire until three in the afternoon. Then, according to Cobb's report, six pieces began working. Under this protective fire a Union brigade, composed mostly of Vermonters, left the banks of the Warwick and crossed the stream at the dam in front of the position held by the Fifteenth North Carolina Regiment. To the left of this unit was the Second Louisiana, to the right were the Sixteenth Georgia, the Eleventh Georgia (it had replaced the Twenty-fourth Georgia), and Tom Cobb's Georgia Legion.

The attackers, for a time under the personal direction of McClellan, succeeded in putting three companies across the stream. A hot fight ensued during which the Federals forced their way into the rifle pits of the Fifteenth North Carolina, whose commander, Colonel Robert M. McKinney, was killed. Thereupon, the men broke and general confusion prevailed. At this point, according to General Magruder's battle report, Cobb "in person rallied the troops under a terrific fire, and by his voice and his example entirely re-established their steadiness." Cobb's own report of the Battle of Lee's Mill made no such precise claim. It did, however, give special recognition to the Seventh Georgia Regiment and to Colonel G. T. Anderson "for successful movements of the extreme left of my command."

For three hours the Battle of Lee's Mill raged. Twice was the enemy repulsed and finally driven back across the Warwick River, and beyond the range of Cobb's one useful artillery piece—a second had been disabled and the third could not be fired without endangering his own infantry. Cobb estimated enemy losses at two hundred, including killed, wounded, and prisoners. Magruder reckoned three times that number. The Federals admitted the loss of less than two hundred. Cobb's report did not give the number of his own losses, but he wrote his wife that the figure did not exceed ninety; Magruder thought it was not in excess of seventy-five.

Cobb was proud of his part in the Battle of Lee's Mill. He was particularly elated at the notice the engagement received in the North, one newspaper there reporting the presence of General McClellan in the company of Prince de Joinville. "When the fight caused an investigation by the federal congress—and was conducted by the Commander in Chief of their army—it begins to assume an important character," was his boast a month after the engagement. Only a minor brush in McClellan's month-long siege of Yorktown, it was Cobb's first significant test under fire. An ego that had long been sustained by favorable election returns had now found a suitable substitute.[15]

Northern concern over the Battle of Lee's Mill was not the only satisfaction for Brigadier-General Cobb. He and some others viewed it as a vindication of "political" generals, whose feud with West Pointers had not abated. For the moment Cobb offered them some comfort. His brother-in-law thought the expression, "handled the troops under his command with consummate skill," would read strange to General Braxton Bragg and other intransigent graduates of the U. S. Military Academy on the Hudson.[16]

It is therefore understandable why Cobb became upset weeks later when an effort was made to deprive him of the honor of the "victory" at Lee's Mill.[17] Colonel Anderson, whom he had credited with stabilizing his left, was alleged to have inspired a story denying Cobb's presence during the action of April 16. This version, which appeared in the Richmond *Dispatch*, ascribed to Anderson the repulsion of the enemy. Such a claim "exceeds Munchausen in his best days," was Cobb's estimate of Anderson's role.

---

[15] Summarized from Cobb's battle report (MS.), April 22, to McLaws; McLaws' and Magruder's reports in *Official Reports of Battles*, 501-510; *ORA*, 1 Series, XI, pt. 1, 363-379, 403-423, 445; George B. McClellan, *McClellan's Own Story* (New York, 1887), 285; Cobb to his wife, Apr. 18, May 14, 1862.

[16] John B. Lamar to Cobb, April 28, 1862.

[17] McClellan also claimed a "victory" (McClellan, 286).

The explanation, he wrote his wife on May 17, "is that *Col.* Anderson wants to be *Genl.* Anderson." Who was behind this claim to discredit his military ability? He suspected Robert Toombs, who, according to Tom Cobb, was at this time "drinking like a fish and making an ass of himself."[18]

Howell Cobb well understood his fiery colleague from Georgia, noting that Colonel Anderson was one of his brigade commanders. He added facetiously in a letter to Mrs. Cobb, May 17, that, even though Toombs had not arrived at Lee's Mill until the day after the fight, he might well decide in time to demand for himself the credit he had already claimed for his subordinate.

For more than two weeks after the engagement at Lee's Mill, Cobb's men served almost continuously in the trenches along the Yorktown-Warwick line. Constant rain kept them knee-deep in mud and water; the weather was exceedingly cold; fires were forbidden; and McClellan's artillery and infantry played on them day and night. On May 3 General Johnston pulled his army out of the line, regrouped it at Williamsburg, about fifteen miles up the Peninsula from Yorktown, and on May 5 engaged the enemy in a stiff rear-guard action there. Cobb's brigade, now in Magruder's division, missed this fight, because on May 4 Magruder, reduced to a division commander in mid-April, had been ordered to continue his retreat toward Richmond.[19]

On May 13 Cobb wrote his wife that the entire Confederate Army had taken a position about twenty miles from Richmond, and that both President Davis and General Lee had on that date visited and conferred with its ranking generals. Inasmuch as he belonged to "the *fourth tier*

[18] T. R. R. Cobb to his wife, May 16, 1862 (Cobb Letters). Toombs' private correspondence of this time reveals an intense dislike for Davis, Lee, and Johnston. He claimed that Davis and his West Point generals, Beauregard excepted, had brought the Confederacy to the verge of ruin. He boasted that he could end the war in one day, if permitted to order the army to fight. See Robert Toombs to his wife, May 13, 17, 1862 (in Toombs Papers, University of Georgia Library, Athens) and Toombs to Stephens, May 17, 1862 (Phillips, 594).

[19] *Official Reports of Battles*, 506; McClellan, 288; Freeman, I, 174, 193.

Brigadiers," he was not invited to the discussion and was thus unable to report its decision. In this and other conferences the Confederate high command determined to hold Richmond at all costs. While General McClellan had all along suspected this to be the case, his extreme sense of caution served as a drag on his military judgment until Howell Cobb unwittingly freed him. On June 15 Cobb assured one of McClellan's officers, with whom he was then conferring on the matter of prisoner exchanges, that while in his judgment the decision to hold Richmond was foolish, the Yankees could have the Capital City only after the Rebels had voluntarily elected to abandon it.

During the last weeks of May Johnston drew his army of over fifty thousand men closer to Richmond in anticipation of a Federal assault. Cobb's brigade was moved to the southern bank of the Chickahominy River, about four miles from Richmond and about an equal distance below the Mechanicsville Bridge. Here it was quartered at Camp Clover on May 26. Describing the vicinity of his new encampment as "the most beautiful country in the world," on May 26 he wrote his wife that the enemy was across the river "and we have the mutual pleasure of looking at each other during the day—and keeping an equally close watch during the night. No one knows how or when the contest is to commence, but I suppose it must be in a few days. Our army is full of hope & spirit & I do not doubt the result." The rapid retreat up the Peninsula had not been a pleasant experience. For one thing, rations could not be regularly distributed and Cobb complained that his men had at times behaved imprudently. "If you give them four days rations & direct them to cook it—they will eat it up in twenty-four hours." Even so, he believed most of his men lived better in the army than they had at home. Not only were they hopeful and high spirited, but, he reported, their health was better than it had been when they left Yorktown.[20]

[20] *ORA*, 1 Series, XI, pt. 1, 1054; *ibid.*, 1 Series, XI, pt. 3, 229-230, 530-531.

The blow Cobb had been expecting fell on May 31: General Johnston attacked the enemy a few miles southeast of Richmond at Seven Pines. He hoped to overwhelm them before reinforcements could be brought up. For some reason he did not use Magruder's division, the largest in his command. Consequently, Cobb's brigade did not go into action. On June 1, the day the Battle of Seven Pines ended, President Davis appointed General Lee to succeed General Johnston, the latter having been seriously wounded the day before. For at least ten days afterwards the Second Brigade remained on the Chickahominy. Cobb described the situation as stalemate. With the river swollen, the two armies stood "looking at each other, without being able to advance." Nonetheless, he was kept busy, visiting his lines, keeping his pickets at their posts, fortifying his position, and making plans to negotiate with Colonel Thomas M. Key of McClellan's army on the delicate subject of prisoner exchanges.

On June 12 the Second moved to a position on Nine Mile Road, thus putting it more directly to the east of Richmond and a short distance south of the Chickahominy. Although the records do not reveal the precise location of the new encampment, it may be assumed from an order which Cobb sent his regimental commanders that his brigade had been sent to the scene of the late battle to clear away the debris. His order was to clean up the neighborhood of what he jocosely referred to as "Camp Comfort." "All offensive matter" was to be removed or buried in the interest of his men's health. Within a week Cobb's own health became a matter of concern. His doctor prescribed quinine pills, which he kept in his pocket for several days, and "such was their efficiency that I feel greatly relieved without the necessity of swallowing them."

Except for Williamsburg and Seven Pines, there had been very little fighting during the retreat from Yorktown. Because Magruder's division had not been used in either of these battles, Cobb's Second Brigade missed both of them. Why General Johnston had not used his largest division is not clear. The Cobb brothers, both of whom were devoted to "Prince John," believed Generals Johnston and Lee, and perhaps others, wished to get rid of the "Old Hero." Tom Cobb reported that Magruder had twice been ordered to the Southwest, had begged off each time, but finally on June 18 had agreed to go, if the Cobb brothers would go with him.

Magruder remained with Lee's army long enough, however, to take part in the spectacular Seven Days' Battle (June 25-July 1) which was to end the three-months' Peninsular campaign. Ordered on June 29 to pursue the Federals, who were falling back to their new base at Harrison's Landing on the James, Magruder displayed a fatal timidity and thereby may have lost an opportunity to remain with the Army of Northern Virginia. His behavior greatly influenced that of his good friend, Howell Cobb. However, the records are so sketchy as to render Cobb's part in the last three days of the battle far from clear. His own report is erroneously dated June 12, and, although brief, offers the best source of information on the performance of the Second Brigade.

Alerted several days before June 29, the date Magruder received orders to take after the retreating Federals, Cobb's men had spent the preceding night in the trenches of "Burnt Chimney" on Nine Mile Road. Leaving this position, they had moved almost due east to a point near Savage Station. There, late in the afternoon, they had engaged the enemy in a stiff encounter. The pursuit, however, had not been swift enough. McClellan had slipped away early the next day to the protection of his guns on Malvern Hill. Lee had then removed Magruder from the chase and shifted him to a position on the Confederate right. Cobb reported that his brigade continued the pursuit on June 30 and July 1. However, it would appear that he mistook the maneuver to the right, which had involved him in considerable marching and counter-marching, as a continuation of the mission of June 29. He had left "Burnt Chimney" on June 29 with some twenty-seven hundred men.

They had been called on to do an excessive amount of
marching that day and the next. In fact, they were so busy
marching during these two days that they could find no
time to eat. Consequently, when they reached the ground
that had been assigned to them near Crew's Farm, less than
fifteen hundred of them were able to participate in the
assault on Malvern Hill on July 1.

The Second Brigade's position in front of Malvern Hill
was to the right of Brigadier-General Lewis Armistead's.
Three regiments were posted in as many different locations,
thus, in Cobb's own words, "rendering my own position . . .
an embrassing one." His main contribution to the fighting
of July 1 was the assistance he furnished Armistead, whose
position he described as "the most advanced." General Lee
was to credit him with helping to drive enemy parties under
their guns. But the price Cobb had paid was exceedingly
high. Of his men who had charged the batteries on Malvern Hill, one-third were killed or wounded.[21]

Thus ended the controversial Peninsular campaign. Back
home, disappointed civilians grumbled. "The whole story,"
wrote Mrs. Cobb on July 13, "is that Gen. Magruder, Gen.
Toombs, and Gen. Cobb were *drunk* upon the battlefield."[22]
Augusta and the whistle stops along the Georgia Rail Road
were seething with this rumor. To the frustrated homefolks,
who were looking for a scapegoat, the wildest rumor gained
almost immediate acceptance. For example, in Milledgeville the *Southern Federal Union* asserted that several
generals had been drunk during the battles around Richmond; in Macon the *Georgia Telegraph*, July 22, deplored
the drunkeness that had enabled McClellan to escape. Even

[21] Summarized from *Reports of the Operations of the Army of
Northern Virginia* . . . (Richmond, 1864), I, 276-279; Freeman, I,
225-259, 538-556; *ORA*, 1 Series, XI, pt. 1, 1064-1065; *ibid.*, 1 Series,
XI, pt. 2, 956-957; *ibid.*, 1 Series, XI, pt. 3, 530-531; *ibid.*, 2 Series,
III, 674-675, 983; Warren W. Hassler, Jr., *General George B.
McClellan* . . . (Baton Rouge, 1957), 158-166; T. R. R. Cobb to his
wife, June 19, 1862 (Cobb Letters); Cobb to his wife, June 19, 1862.
[22] E. J. Eldridge, surgeon of the Sixteenth Georgia Regiment, declared on Aug. 4, 1862 that, if Magruder had been under the influence
of liquor on July 1, he in no way revealed it to him (*ORA*, 1 Series,
XI, pt. 2, 682-683).

Tom Cobb, still on the Peninsula, denounced General Lee as "haughty and boorish and supercilious in his bearing." Howell's eldest son wrote: "I am tired of the war."

Howell himself was indisposed, dejected, and planned soon to leave Virginia to regain his health.[23] His illness was disturbing to no less a person than General Lee, for it threatened to upset his search for a formula for prisoner exchanges. Two days after the Battle of Malvern Hill he had urged Secretary of War Randolph to re-open negotiations with Federal authorities for a general exchange. The large number of prisoners taken during the last week of the campaign created difficulties which Lee hoped to ease by an exchange agreement. Howell Cobb had previously engaged in prisoner exchange conferences with Federal officers and Lee believed he was now the logical man to resume talks on the subject. Although he knew the Georgian to be too ill for field duty, Lee hoped he would be able to undertake this important assignment.

Cobb's experience with the delicate problem of prisoner exchanges went back to February 18, at which time Secretary of War Benjamin had authorized him to go to Norfolk to confer with General John E. Wool. Five days later the Cobb-Wool talks began. They dragged on until March 1, ending in stalemate. Cobb was actually relieved by their failure. He wrote his wife a few days afterwards: "I don't think a worse thing could be done than to provide for the immediate restoration of prisoners to their homes. It would be an invitation to our army to surrender as it would restore the men to their homes and relieve them of further military duty until exchanged. This would suit drafted men exactly and would be a strong temptation to a good many others."

After the failure of the Cobb-Wool talks, the issue of a general exchange of prisoners was not raised again until July 8, when General McClellan proposed one to General

[23] T. R. R. Cobb to his wife, July 8, 11, John A. Cobb to Lucy [Barrow] July 4, 1862 (Cobb Letters); *Southern Banner*, July 23, 1862.

Lee. Lee immediately went into action, recommending that the War Department accept the offer. A few days later he wrote McClellan that he had appointed Cobb to meet with the proper Union officers and arrange for an exchange "upon terms of perfect equality." Meanwhile, McClellan had chosen Colonel Thomas M. Key to meet Cobb. Soon afterwards, the rival commanders arranged for their official representatives to meet alone on June 15 at a point near the Mechanicsville Bridge.

Accordingly, Cobb and Key spent four hours together in a shanty near the place designated. Key was impressed with Cobb's courteous manner, his free and earnest conversation, and his neat uniform. The Union field officer of the day, J. H. Simpson, who had known Cobb before the war, failed to recognize him "because of the great length and color of his beard (it was brown, as if burned by the sun). . . ." The Georgian eased Simpson's embarrassment with the remark: "Yes, we all seem to be fighting under masked faces." According to official reports, the conferees discussed other matters than exchange of prisoners. At least some of their time was given to ways and means of getting peace. When the Union officer raised this subject, Cobb replied at length that peace could be had at any time "within half an hour" by a recognition of separation. "We must," said he, "be independent or conquered." Key's rejoinder was that the only possible peace formula was submission by the South and amnesty by the Federal government. The Confederate officer was reported to have answered that any Southern leader who advocated such a proposition would be slain at once. Key argued that the South was dis-united, that secession had been the work of the ruling planters, and warned that they would have to be supplanted by "laboring and middle class white men who would be loyal" to the Union. To these remarks Cobb was reported to have replied "with much excitement" that none could be found in the "original states" of the Confederacy, who could be made into a loyal class. Key's somewhat ominous rejoinder was that many such people were there and others would go "on our invitation."[24]

While nothing of consequence on the subject of prisoner exchanges came from the Cobb-Key conference, both Key and McClellan were momentarily disposed to believe otherwise. On the other hand, Secretary of War Stanton was highly displeased at Key's failure to confine his conversation to the subject for which the conference had been called. He therefore reprimanded the officer and wrote McClellan that the matter now rested with President Lincoln. This was the situation on July 3, when Lee urged Cobb to resume negotiations. The Georgian's poor health compelled him to decline the responsibility.

A few days after the Battle of Malvern Hill Cobb was in Richmond; on July 12 he was granted a thirty-day leave to recover his health.[25] Four days later he had arrived in Athens, Georgia, where in the quiet of his home he was reported as improving.[26] He now had time for reflection. His thoughts were naturally on the Confederate war effort. Wherein was it faulty? On this subject he had two noteworthy ideas. He would end the "unpopular—almost odious" conscription, substituting for it either state quotas or a scheme to authorize the formation of companies, or larger units, to be tendered the President. Either would provide more recruits than the conscript law. And, second, he would also stop the practice of impressing Negroes to help build fortifications. They were needed to do the much more important work of collecting fodder and corn to sustain the army. These were the views of a seasoned politician and

[24] *ORA*, 1 Series, XI, pt. 1, 1052-1056; *ibid.*, 2 Series, III, 663, 800-801, 812-913, 893; 2 Series, IV, 14, 31, 48, 773, 797-798; 2 Series, V, 21-22. See also William B. Hesseltine, *Civil War Prisons* . . . (Columbus, 1930), 24-27; Cobb to his wife, March 4, 1862. A Confederate soldier, W. B. C. Coker, wrote his brother, July 28, 1861, that 30,000 handcuffs had been captured at the First Battle of Manassas which 'they [Yankees] intended to put on us and take us over to Washington" (in Heidler Collection, University of Georgia Library, Athens).

[25] Jno. Withers to Cobb, July 12, 1862.

[26] John A. Cobb to John B. Lamar, July 17, 1862; *Southern Banner*, July 23, 1862.

veteran of the Peninsular campaign.   To Secretary of War
Randolph he forwarded them before returning, improved
in health, to the Army of Northern Virginia.[27]

[27] *ORA,* 4 Series, II, 34-35.

CHAPTER IV

The Maryland Invasion

THE MONTH WITH FRIENDS and relatives in Athens had passed quickly and happily, but it was with no little satisfaction that Brigadier-General Howell Cobb rejoined his brigade, then encamped on the James River about twelve miles from Richmond.[1] The next day, August 18, he was in the saddle at an early hour, riding with General McLaws in search of McClellan's army. Tired and hungry the two seekers returned to camp at 9:30 P.M., convinced that "McClelland [sic] had 'skedaddled'."[2]

Actually, the Union commander had been ordered back to the Potomac River to reinforce General John Pope, who had now decided to take Richmond by the overland route.[3] Meanwhile, General Lee had turned the main body of his army northward to intercept him. Cobb's brigade, now in McLaws' division which, with D. H. Hill's and John G. Walker's, was hastening northward to join Lee's forces.[4] On August 23 Cobb's brigade arrived at Hanover Junction, some thirty miles north of Richmond. On that day Cobb wrote his wife that he had spent the night before "in the open air, with my head pillowed against a tree, & refreshed during the night with the constant fall of rain. This morning I had no dry clothing as my wagons had not arrived, &

<hr>

[1] *Southern Banner*, Aug. 12, 1862; Cobb to his wife, Aug. 16, 1862.
[2] John A. Cobb to Lucy [Barrow], Aug. 18, Cobb to his wife, Aug. 19, 1862.
[3] See T. Harry Williams, *Lincoln and His Generals* (New York, 1952), 144-152.
[4] Freeman, II, 145, 719.

so I spent the day in my saddle & before my wagons arrived I was dry and comfortable."

By covering sixty miles during the next three and one-half days Cobb's men made camp on August 28 at Rapidan Station.[5] Cobb himself was so exhausted at the end of this swift march that his normally pleasant disposition gave way to resentment. In bitter words to his wife he conveyed his feelings. No troops, he complained on August 29, had ever had a harder march, nor had ever a march been so poorly directed, "owing to the fact that it was conducted by Maj. Genl. D. H. Hill . . . , a weak, self-conceited heartless & cruel ass." Had it been possible to get a fair trial, Cobb added, he would have charged him "with incapacity & inhumanity—and relieve the service of as despicable a wretch, as ever disgraced any army." If he had to continue in Hill's command, he continued, he would be tempted to resign rather than tolerate "his folly and meanness." The two younger Cobbs, John A. and Howell, Jr., were equally bitter, the latter, who as a student at the University of Georgia had not always been in favor of his professors, characterizing Hill as "a selfish brute."[6] The elder Cobb also recorded some of the appalling statistics of the "inhuman" march from Hanover Junction. "Men," he wrote, "absolutely fell & died on the side of the road from the heat—one case I know of & I have heard of others." The Georgia Legion, which had started with 500 men on August 13, numbered only 313. Of the approximately two thousand men in his brigade when the march began, Cobb believed only about thirteen hundred would be fit to go on. Included in these estimates were deserters who, unable to endure the hardships, had absented themselves in the night. Cobb sent a list of these men to his son, Lamar, asking him to ascertain specific causes and to notify those able to return that they would be "advertised & treated as deserters."[7]

[5] John A. Cobb to Lucy [Barrow], Aug. 28, 1862.
[6] Howell Cobb, Jr. to his mother, Aug. 29, 1862. Hill had taught at Washington College, Lexington, Va. and at Davidson College, N. C.
[7] Cobb to his wife, Aug. 29, John A. Cobb to Lucy [Barrow], Aug. 18, 1862.

On August 30 Cobb's brigade began the next leg of its northward advance, from Rapidan Station to Leesburg. Early in September it passed the scene of the Second Battle of Manassas (August 29-30), a furious contest in which Lee had won a brilliant victory over Pope. The horrible wreckage in human life that had been wrought there was not yet cleared away, as Cobb's men passed. As one Confederate soldier reported, "The Yankees lay . . . rotting and *stinking*, their *heads* and *forms* swelled to twice the natural size & *black as negroes*. I would fain pray that I might never behold such a sight again, but of that I cannot tell."[8] What they saw there gave new hope to Cobb's men, one of them writing his sweetheart that his next letter would be sent from Baltimore or Philadelphia. This young man was confident the enemy would not fight again. The struggle, he assured his darling, would soon be over and he would "never be in a hurry to get into another war."[9]

On September 5 a rumor reached Georgia that Brigadier-General Cobb had been killed at Second Manassas. In Leesburg the next day he was, of course, very much alive, reporting that this Virginia town was to be the assembly point for the Maryland invasion. The Southern press, and other sources as well, had been vigorously urging such action since Second Manassas. Lee also believed the time had arrived to invade the enemy's country and Cobb thought the Confederate commander was now pushing his men especially hard in order to take advantage of the "greatly demoralized" Federal army. Confederate *esprit de corps,* on the other hand, was the "finest," Cobb believed. He was particularly proud of the response of his men to every trial. Across the Potomac there were soon to be more trials. Cobb and his men now headed that way to confront them, reaching the vicinity of Frederick, Maryland, on September 9.

Cobb thought the invading army was on its way to Baltimore or to some point between that city and Washing-

---

[8] F. M. Coker to his wife, Sept. 8, 1862 (Heidler Collection).
[9] John A. Cobb to Lucy [Barrow], Sept. 4, 1862.

ton. Lee, he reasoned, was preparing to cut all rail communications to the Federal capital from the north. However, he understood that before any movement Lee planned to send a peace proposal to Major-General Henry W. Halleck, the new Federal commander, offering to lay down his arms in return for recognition of the independence of the Confederacy. Cobb was convinced that nothing would come of such a proffer, "for the Yankee Government is not yet prepared to recognize our independence."

Of more immediate concern were the people of Maryland. Cobb could detect no real evidence of feeling for the South among them. Lee was extremely circumspect in dealing with them, especially with those of Frederick. They had warned that their shops would be closed, if Confederates overran the town. Anxious to replenish his dwindling supplies, Lee deferred to their wishes by ordering all officers and men to stay out of the town, except those on business.[10] As a result, the Confederates were well behaved during their sojourn in Maryland, although not so naive as one of their officers reported. According to Lieutenant F. M. Coker, several of his men were seen conversing with some women in Middletown, who from a porch were talking loudly and gesticulating profusely. A "Southern citizen" who was passing by asked the officer why his men were speaking to such persons. For $2.50, he observed with a note of rebuke, he could "sleep all night with either of them." Coker's apologetic reply was that such women were not so plentiful in the South and consequently Southern boys could not distinguish them so readily. "And such are hundreds of our opposers in Maryland and Northern Va.," continued the young Georgia Lieutenant, "poor devils who have nothing themselves, & envy those who do have—infernal foreigners, fit only for *slaves* and lives of vice and crime. Irish and *Dutch* by the thousand."[11]

Near Frederick on September 9 General Lee made the

[10] Mrs. Cobb to Cobb, Sept. 7, Cobb to his wife, Sept. 6, 9, 1862; *Southern Federal Union*, Sept. 9, 1862.
[11] F. M. Coker to his wife, Oct. 5, 1862 (Heidler Collection).

momentous decision to divide his army—one part to go to
Hagerstown, the other to envelop the Union force at
Harpers Ferry. Between the Confederate Army and its
twin objectives lay South Mountain, extending almost due
northward from the Potomac River across Maryland and
into Pennsylvania. Numerous passes offered access to the
region beyond. One of them, Crampton's Gap, was destined
to become the scene of a bloody fight involving Howell
Cobb's brigade. West of the mountain was Pleasant Valley.
Beyond rose Elk Ridge Mountain, whose southern tip,
Maryland Heights, stood like a sentinel before Harpers
Ferry, nestled near the junction of the Shenandoah and
Potomac rivers. Maryland Heights extended slightly eastward along the northern bank of the Potomac until it almost
touched the southern end of South Mountain. Directly
below and opposite Harpers Ferry was Sandy Hook. Elk
Ridge Mountain, Maryland Heights, and South Mountain
formed a U-shaped ridge, the control of which was neces-
sary for the success of the Confederate operation against
Harpers Ferry.

It was General "Stonewall" Jackson who drew the assignment of taking Harpers Ferry. He in turn gave McLaws
six additional brigades, making a total of ten, and ordered
him to occupy Maryland Heights by September 12.[12] Leaving Frederick on the tenth, McLaws reached Pleasant
Valley the next day, crossing South Mountain at Brownsville Gap. For the operation against Maryland Heights he
chose two of his best brigades. The others remained behind to protect his rear from enemy thrusts through the
passes of South Mountain, and his left from the Union
force at Harpers Ferry, in case it escaped and broke into
Pleasant Valley. With the main task progressing nicely,
McLaws decided on a precautionary move to protect his left.
On the thirteenth, therefore, he ordered Cobb to take his
brigade down Pleasant Valley, round the Heights, and to
occupy Sandy Hook. The Georgian accomplished this task
quickly and without serious opposition. At 10:00 P.M. on

[12] *ORA*, 1 Series, XIX, pt. 2, 603.

the day Sandy Hook was occupied, McLaws received word from headquarters that an enemy force was coming up fast from the east to relieve Harpers Ferry. Unfortunately, Confederate generals had developed the habit of subjecting such intelligence to considerable discount, especially if the Union commander happened to be General McClellan, as in this case it was, for he had lately been restored to the Army of the Potomac. Even so, McLaws believed that he was ready; surely, his soldiery instincts had not played him false. Cobb would protect his left and seven brigades were standing by to plug the gaps in South Mountain. Thus, on September 14 he set to work to complete the occupation of Maryland Heights.

Meanwhile, to the east of Frederick the Federal forces began to show signs of life. On the afternoon of September 13 McClellan discovered Lee's battle plan. With unusual speed he pressed toward South Mountain in hope of striking before the two units of the Confederate Army could be joined. Thus, as McLaws was preparing to complete his mission on Maryland Heights, he was suddenly threatened with disaster from the gaps of South Mountain. McClellan had arrived in force. Quickly, McLaws set to work to plug the gaps. It was a difficult task, because he knew so little of the local topography. First, he rushed Brigadier-General Paul Semmes with two brigades back through Brownsville Gap, from whence he had passed two days before. Suddenly, another pass, Crampton's Gap, was discovered about two miles to the north. To it Semmes sent Colonel William Parham with William Mahone's brigade. Learning that this force was inadequate, McLaws now called Cobb to come up from Sandy Hook.

Cobb received the order at one o'clock in the afternoon of September 14 to hasten to Brownsville Gap. Arriving three hours later, he was handed another message from Colonel Thomas T. Munford, urging him to bring his brigade to Crampton's Gap at once to help relieve excessive pressure. Immediately, Cobb directed two of his regiments to that point. Before he could get them off, he received another

call, however; this one was from Parham, who reported
that the enemy drive was gathering momentum. Cobb
personally accompanied his remaining two regiments to the
battle site. In route he received yet another message, this
one from McLaws, himself busily engaged in pushing ahead
with the work on Maryland Heights: "Hold the Gap, if it
costs the life of every man in [*your*] command."

Now duly impressed with the gravity of the situation,
Cobb moved ahead "with the utmost dispatch," entered
Crampton's Gap, and amidst great disorder managed to
get his men to the top of South Mountain. He observed
that Parham, who had recently driven the enemy's center
down the eastern slope, was having trouble, the extent of
which momentarily escaped the Georgian. His first reaction, he later reported, was that the Federal effort to
clear the area had failed. However, he quickly discovered
that Parham's flanks were under heavy attack. With the
assistance of Colonel Munford, he ordered two of his regiments to the right and two to the left to meet what was
rapidly threatening to become an enveloping action. As the
Confederate line seemed to stablize, the center, which extended down the eastern slope, began to cave in. Then the
entire line started to waver. With the situation steadily
worsening, Cobb, aided by Semmes' Tenth Georgia, tried
to rally his men, but they broke and, according to Munford,
fled down the western slope of South Mountain like "a
flock of frightened sheep." By nightfall several hundred
of them managed to reach Pleasant Valley. This was the
situation when McLaws, his mission on Maryland Heights
finished, arrived with General J. E. B. Stuart. Overwhelmed with grief, Cobb greeted them with these words:
"Dismount, gentlemen, dismount, if your lives are dear to
you! The enemy is within fifty yards of us; I am expecting their attack every minute. Oh, my dear Stuart,
that I should live to experience such a disaster! What can
be done? What can save us?"

After clearing Crampton's Gap, the Federals temporarily
halted. Thus, during the night McLaws was able to form

a line across Pleasant Valley less than two miles below to
protect the roads leading to Harpers Ferry, which had
fallen to Jackson the day before. Despite the capture of
that strategic point, the Confederate situation was desperate, for what had happened at Crampton's Gap had been
duplicated at the passes to the north. Lee was now compelled to regroup his forces earlier than he had planned,
thus setting the stage for the impending Battle of Antietam.
Because of the condition of his troops Cobb did not get
them to the battlefield in time to take part in that engagement, however.

After the disaster at Crampton's Gap, Cobb estimated
that approximately twenty-two hundred Confederates had
engaged seven times as many Federals. Among the former
were thirteen hundred of Cobb's men. Official reports and
the Georgian's own private correspondence vary widely as
to losses. Three days after the battle he wrote his wife
that only three hundred men answered roll-call on the
morning after the engagement. Four days later he reported to McLaws that it was still impossible to give
casualty figures, because the fate of a large number of
missing men remained unknown. It would appear that the
killed and wounded together numbered between three and
five hundred. Among those fatally wounded was John
B. Lamar, who had joined Cobb's staff a short time before
the Maryland invasion and had been shot whilst near his
commander's side. He died the following day and his body
was taken home by Cobb's two sons.[13]

Lamar's death and the bloody reverse at Crampton's Gap
were cruel blows to the sensitive Cobb. For days after the
battle he was engaged in the grim work of collecting the

---

[13] This summary of the Battle of Crampton's Gap is based primarily
on Cobb's report, supplemented by the following sources: Cobb to
McLaws, Sept. 22, T. M. R. Talcott to McLaws, Sept. 10, (McLaws
Papers); Freeman, II, 173-174, 188, 191; Robert U. Johnson and
Clarence C. Buel (eds.), *Battles and Leaders of the Civil War* (New
York, 1888), II, 605-606; *ORA*, 1 Series, XIX, pt. 1, 144-153, 812,
826-827; Cobb to his wife, Sept. 17, 24, 1862; Hassler, 245-257;
Reports of the Operations of the Army of Northern Virginia . . . ,
I, 30; II, 89, 107.

remnants of his badly bruised brigade. By September 20 he had taken his men across the Potomac River to Camp Lizzie.[14] There, about two miles from Martinsburg, Virginia, he awaited orders to move southward, meanwhile assuring his wife that his health was good and that the morale of Lee's army was excellent.[15]

He did not disclose to his wife, however, that he had recently undertaken the delicate task of resolving a crisis in his relations with General McLaws. It will be recalled that Colonel Munford had been extremely critical of Cobb's behavior during the late battle. General McLaws had been even more censorious, charging Cobb with failure to understand his responsibility and blistering his fellow-Georgian with abusive language. For days McLaws played the captious critic, complaining that Cobb had been a great "bother" to him during the final stages of the operation on Maryland Heights.

Because he was unwilling to dismiss McLaws' battlefield expletives as a passing aberration, Cobb requested on September 24 that he and his brigade be transferred to another division. Reminding McLaws of his unrefined language, Cobb pointed out that "I have not your respect and confidence as an officer. The personal affront I pass by. My own self-respect forbids that I should serve under an officer who entertains of me such an opinion." McLaws' prompt reply apparently soothed Cobb's feelings, for he immediately withdrew his request for a transfer and promised to forget "the unpleasant feelings with which I have been oppressed for the last two days." Apparently determined to show his fellow-Georgian that he had few peers, when it came to eating humble pie, McLaws concluded the quarrel as follows: "Whatever remarks . . . I have made, which may have been construed as derogatory to you, had no meaning to me and were mere ebulitions of temper, which I am constantly repenting. The lesson you have

[14] During the Maryland campaign Cobb honored his younger children by naming encampments after them.
[15] Cobb to his wife, Sept. 24, 1862.

given me, in the narrow escape I have made in losing the regard of yourself whom I esteem so warmly—I hope will but make me more careful in the future." To confirm his contrition, General McLaws assured Tom Cobb that he would submit a favorable report of Howell's performance at Crampton's Gap.[16]

From Camp Lizzie Cobb moved his men to Camp Tom, about seven miles west of Winchester. Here, on October 6, General Longstreet reviewed McLaws' division. Because of an infected foot, so painful he could not pull a boot over it, Cobb turned his brigade over to his brother Tom. Still nursing his foot four days later, he was cheered by the arrival of new recruits, who were rapidly restoring Lee's army to its previous strength. He was especially delighted with his own command which now numbered 1,600 men, but the stubborn infection kept him inactive. With his brother in charge, he decided to go home about the middle of October. He was destined never to rejoin his comrades in the Army of Northern Virginia.[17]

On his way home Cobb stopped off in Richmond to call on his old friend, William M. Browne, aid-de-camp to President Davis, with whom he discussed the detachment of Cobb's brigade from the Army of Northern Virginia.[18] At any rate, when Cobb reached Augusta on October 23, he tried to get a transfer to Georgia.[19] On October 27 the War Department, acting on direct instructions from General Lee, ordered Cobb to report to General P. G. T. Beauregard, then commandant at Charleston, South Carolina.[20]

Apparently, Cobb was now enjoying good health, although "somewhat reduced."[21] No longer was his physical condition a factor in his desire for a transfer from Mc-

[16] *ORA*, 1 Series, XIX, pt. 1, 818-819, 826-827, 870; Cobb to McLaws and reply, Sept. 24-25 (McLaws Papers); T. R. R. Cobb to his wife (Cobb Letters).
[17] Cobb to his wife, Oct. 4, 6, 10, Tom Barrow to his friend, Nov. 1, 1862.
[18] This is inferred from John A. and Lamar Cobb to their father, Oct. 3, 26, 1862.
[19] D. C. Barrow to John A .Cobb, Oct. 24, 1862.
[20] Lamar Cobb to his father, Oct. 26, 1862; *ORA*, 1 Series, LIII, 262.
[21] *Southern Banner*, Oct. 29, 1862.

Laws' command.[22] Of far greater importance was the Crampton's Gap reverse. Because of it there was little chance of his earning another promotion. This meant that his brother, still a colonel but recognized as the better soldier, would be embarrassed by his continued presence in Lee's army. Outweighing these considerations was Cobb's desire to be closer home. He sincerely needed to look after his family and his finances, for John B. Lamar's death had seriously damaged the Cobb-Lamar business interests.

Their five plantations in Middle and South Georgia needed immediate attention. Cobb planned to have his eldest son, John A., released from the army to manage them. And a military assignment in Georgia or Florida would enable Cobb to supervise his son without neglecting his duty to the Confederacy. On November 1 he wrote his wife that he had hopes of working out such a plan with the authorities.

The attitude of certain Confederate authorities was also a factor in Cobb's transfer. They realized he was a popular figure in the Southeast. If he were sent to that area, he might be able to raise enough troops on the spot to defend it from possible enemy invasion. The plan also seemed to offer the advantage of a minimum of interference with Lee's reorganization of the Army of Northern Virginia.[23] Moreover, as a loyal Davis man, Cobb's presence in the Southeast would serve as a checkrein on the recalcitrant Governor Brown of Georgia, consistent critic of the Richmond authorities. Thus, Cobb's transfer grew out of a combination of personal concern and Confederate military and political considerations. The road ahead was to be as involved as the circumstances which brought the man and his new assignment together.

[22] A. L. Hull to Mary Ann L. Erwin, March 28, 1907 (in Lamar Family History File, University of Georgia Library, Athens).
[23] *ORA*, 1 Series, XIV, 688, 703-705; Freeman, II, 250-268.

CHAPTER V

Commandant of Middle Florida

BRIGADIER-GENERAL COBB used the six weeks' interlude between his detachment from the Army of Northern Virginia and his assumption of duty in the newly-formed Military District of Middle Florida to the fullest advantage. After a short stay in Athens, he went to Macon to look after the family plantations. Neglected since John B. Lamar had left for the Maryland invasion, they required immediate attention. The overseers, long accustomed to taking orders from Lamar, needed a permanent manager. Cobb now began negotiations with the Richmond authorities to have his eldest son, John A., detailed to direct the overseers of the numerous holdings in Sumter and Baldwin counties.[1] (Early in 1863 the son received approval for this duty.)[2] Before leaving Macon, Cobb sold 600 bags of cotton, paid Lamar's debts, and arranged with his overseers to provide Mrs. Cobb with the customary winter's supply of bacon and stuffed sausage.[3]

Meanwhile, his orders caught up with him, and early in November he went to Charleston to confer with General Beauregard about his assignment in Middle Florida.[4] One of seven districts in the Department of South Carolina, Georgia, and Florida, that of Middle Florida had been created late in 1862 at the request of the governors of

[1] John A. Cobb to his father, Dec. 2, 1862.
[2] Undated enclosure with Mrs. Cobb to Cobb, Jan. [?], 1863.
[3] Cobb to his wife, Nov. 10, 1862; *ORA*, 1 Series, XIV, 677.
[4] Mrs. Cobb to Cobb, Nov. 4, 1862.

Georgia, Florida, and Alabama.[5] It embraced the region
between the Suwannee and Choctawhatchee rivers and all
works for the defense of the Apalachicola River and its
main affluents, the Chattahoochee and Flint, and was established primarily to defend the Apalachicola against the
penetration of Federal gunboats. Cobb knew next to
nothing about the military problems involved and in all
likelihood Beauregard was no better equipped. Although
the former characterized their discussion as "fruitful," it
could scarcely have dealt with anything more than the very
general. Beauregard expressed satisfaction with Cobb's
assignment and requested him to draw up and submit as
soon as possible a "concise statement of [the area's] defensive condition & resources."

Shortly afterwards, Cobb departed for Athens and Macon.
Early in December he left the latter city for Columbus,
which, located at the headwaters of the Chattahoochee River
and commanding the rich farming area to the south, he considered second in importance to Richmond. Here old friends
told him much about the district which he was to administer.
He also met Captain Theodore Moreno, an engineer, who
had come up from Florida to give him his first authentic
glimpse of the task ahead. Impressed with the reports of
the paucity of troops in Middle Florida and the suggestions
of Moreno, Cobb wrote both Beauregard and President
Davis, urging them to send him more men and requesting in
particular his old regiment, the Sixteenth Georgia. Around
it he proposed to found a suitable military force.

While still in Columbus, Cobb and Moreno drew up a
specific plan of defense for Middle Florida. It embraced
two separate projects. In the first place, Cobb proposed
sinking obstructions in the Apalachicola River which, flowing almost due south for seventy-five miles from Georgia's
southwestern corner to the Gulf of Mexico, traversed Cobb's
district slightly east of its greatest width. With this means
of ingress sealed, Cobb believed the only remaining pos-
sibility of penetration was overland across the waist of

[5] Candler, III, 314-315.

Middle Florida, east of the Apalachicola and adjacent to
that part of the Gulf known as Apalachee Bay. Emptying
into the bay was the St. Mark's River with the town of St.
Mark's near its mouth. Some seventy miles south of
Tallahassee, St. Mark's was joined to the latter by the
Tallahassee Rail Road. If the enemy should be allowed
to force a landing there, the Apalachicola's proposed ob-
structions could be by-passed and the whole of Middle
Florida and Southwest Georgia would be lost. It was to
meet this contingency that Cobb had requested more troops.
Such were the plans Moreno took from Columbus to
Beauregard's headquarters in Charleston.[6]

With his "horses & plunder" loaded on a boat, Cobb
started dowstream on December 4, bound for Quincy,
headquarters for the District of Middle Florida. Some
twenty miles from Chattahoochee, near the forks of the
Apalachicola, the town was about midway between that
city and Tallahassee. Three days later, Cobb was in the
Florida capital, where he conferred with Governor John
Milton and Brigadier-General Joseph Finegan, commander
of the Military District of East Florida.[7] On December 9
he spoke to a joint session of the state legislature, eulogiz-
ing Florida's soldiers and their wives and children, denouncing the "extortioners . . . as the greatest enemy we
have," and exhorting the lawmakers to protect the wives
and children of "our noble defenders" from "this vile and
loathsome class." He promised "to defend successfully
every exposed point and thus secure Georgia, as well as
Florida, against any raids the enemy may contemplate."
One Georgia editor described his efforts as eloquent and
commended him for rebuking extortioners and speculators,
and his adjutant, Captain James Barrow, thought the
Floridians were glad to see their new commander. What
he saw was only a picket "to warn us when to leave."[8]

---

[6] *ORA*, 1 Series, XIV, 684, 697-698, 735, 736; Cobbs order, Jan. [?],
1863; Cobb to his wife, Aug. 7, Dec. 3, 1863.
[7] James Barrow to John A. Cobb, Dec. 7, 1862.
[8] Florida *House Journal*, 1862, 235; Milledgeville (Ga.) *Confederate
Union*, Dec. 23, 1862; James Barrow to John A. Cobb, Dec. 7, 1862.

By temperament and background Howell Cobb was well suited for the duties of district commander. He had a capacity for military administration that had not escaped his superiors. Just a few weeks before he reached Florida, for example, President Davis had assured Governor Milton that the newly-formed military district of Middle Florida was to be in competent hands.[9] Conversely, Cobb's ability as a field officer above brigade commander was open to question. The assignment to Middle Florida, therefore, gave solace to both Cobb and the Confederate authorities.

The governors of Georgia, Florida, and Alabama had been visibly disturbed over the failure of General Finegan at Jacksonville and General John H. Forney at Mobile to provide for the defense of the Apalachicola River country.[10] Speaking early in November, 1862 for the three state executives, Governor John Gill Shorter of Alabama had stressed to President Davis the value of this area to the war effort. Not only did it produce cotton, cattle, hogs, and corn, but within its confines were the two important cities of Tallahassee and Columbus, as well as a long coastline where salt manufacturing was a thriving business.[11] Shorter had insisted that there was danger of an immediate attack and proposed that the area be defended by having the three states raise and turn over to the President several regiments of six-months' volunteers from among those persons not subject to conscription.[12] Only one month afterwards the President had created the new district and ordered its commander there for duty. Cobb quickly discovered that there were less than one thousand troops in the entire district. Scattered between the Suwannee and Choctawhatchee rivers, they possessed no organization above that of a company and had but a single field officer. Captain Barrow thought it would require at least a month to put the district in order. Cobb lost no time in describing his plight to General Beauregard, calling for 5,000 men to

[9] ORA, 1 Series, LIII, 266.
[10] Candler, III, 214-315.
[11] ORA, 1 Series, XV, 946-948.
[12] Candler, III, 214-315. The draft age was 35 to 45.

protect salt works and the rich crops. He drafted a plan
which granted him power to call on the governors of the
three states for quotas and asked Beauregard's approval
of it. Included was the right to call all men subject to
conscription, once an "odious" practice to Cobb, but one
necessary now in order to "stimulate and greatly expedite
the raising of troops."

While his proposal was on its way to Charleston, Cobb
left Quincy for St. Mark's on his first inspection tour. To
General Beauregard he reported on December 11 that the
St. Mark's River channel was too narrow and difficult for
successful passage. Although he ordered the fort there
strengthened, he believed that, if the enemy were to attempt
to move inland from this area, he would by-pass St. Mark's.
From there Cobb went to the Apalachicola River, believed
to be the most likely route of invasion from the Gulf of
Mexico. Because it led to the heart of Middle Florida,
this stream became the object of concentrated defense
operations. Two points were therefore selected and the
installation of appropriate obstructions and batteries was
begun. One was at Rock Bluff, less than twenty miles
below the junction of the Chattahoochee and Flint, and the
other farther south at the Narrows.[13] At least one more
defensive position was to be added on the river and later
the process was to be extended along its forks to give protection to Columbus as well as Southeast Alabama and
Southwest Georgia.[14]

The obstruction of the channel was accomplished by suspending a heavy chain across the river in such a way as to
halt logs, trees, and trash brought downstream by freshets.[15]
Although much of the preliminary work at the early sites
had been completed before the end of 1862, it was not until
late winter that enough rubbish had been caught to close
the channel. Near each encumbrance batteries were em-

[13] *ORA*, 1 Series, XIV, 697-698, 703-710, 728-735; James Barrow to
John A. Cobb, Dec. 7, 1862.
[14] *ORA*, 1 Series, XXVIII, pt. 2, 189-190, 279; John A. Davis to
Cobb, May 8, and Cobb to his wife, Aug. 7, 1863.
[15] Moreno to Cobb, March 1, 1863.

placed to command the approaches from downstream. What Cobb saw on his first visit to the Apalachicola River pleased him, and his report to Charleston brought the reply that General Beauregard was "abundantly satisfied as to the soundness" of the operation. With his report Cobb sent a request for the C. S. S. *Chattahoochee* to assist with river defenses. The request was granted and a few months later the gunboat was in service. Captain Moreno wished to employ the *Chattahoochee* as a lookout near the batteries at the Narrows. Because Cobb never had more than thirty-five hundred effective troops in his district, his batteries were always undermanned and lookouts always spread thinly. A surprise attack might well have disrupted the district's defenses. Following a scare induced by a Yankee advance past Fort Gadsden, some twenty miles from the Gulf and a few miles east of the river, to within eighteen miles of the Narrows, Negroes were tried as lookouts at various points along the river. Because they constantly escaped while on duty, they were of limited utility, however.

Cobb kept a fairly close vigil on the Apalachicola River's defenses during the spring and summer of 1863, travelling by boat and buggy from Quincy to the headwaters and thence to Ford Gadsden. These inspection trips often provided weird experiences with balky horses, broken axles, and violent storms. To his wife he reported one storm as frightening him so badly that it cured his dysentery. On one occasion he was "lulled to sleep by the hoarse music of frogs and the hissing of snakes. The snake part of it I was not aware [of] until next morning or I should have done much less sleeping. . . ." But there was also an occasional pleasant experience, such as the sight of orange groves near Fort Gadsden. This suggested the idea of supplying his staff and family with fresh fruit and immediately he bargained for 5,000 oranges. Certainly, he reflected, Florida's climate was preferable to that of the Old Dominion. Except for its incessant spring rains and intense summer heat, Cobb recorded no objection to Florida.

While Cobb and Moreno were erecting defenses on the

upper reaches of the Apalachicola River, the Federals were busy at its mouth, where lay the town of Apalachicola. Off the coast in the adjacent bays, sounds, inlets, and passes were the ships of the Union blockading force. Operating in the channel was the U. S. S. *Brockenborough,* a sloop which served as a relay station for shore-to-ship communications. When certain Apalachicola citizens, bent upon currying favor with Union authorities, were ready to receive Yankee visitors, signals were passed whereupon shore parties promptly boarded launches and headed for what often turned out to be gay affairs. Such parties arrived daily in the city and sometimes a single one would contain as many as four hundred sailors. To deal with this situation Cobb had only a small cavalry detachment, less than one hundred men, known as the Milton Dragoons, and they generally left the community upon the arrival of the rollicking sailors.

The collusion between some of the Apalachicola's citizens and the Yankee blockaders was a menace to the river country's security. Late in 1862 Cobb resorted to drastic measures in the hope of stopping it. All mail service to and from the city as well as other forms of intercourse were suspended. Protests were immediate and savage, some of them going directly to Quincy. It was claimed that Cobb's order had driven a number of people into nearby woods and swamps to escape starvation. One critic, a planter in nearby Franklin County, wrote Cobb that his restrictions would force a large number of persons to seek supplies from the enemy, which many understood to be available in exchange for an oath of allegiance to the Federal government.

Cobb's order did not stop Yankee sailors from visiting Apalachicola. At length, he recommended to both Governor Milton and General Beauregard that the city be occupied by a Confederate force. It was, he explained, the best place from which to defend the river; besides, it was more healthful than any of the upstream sites. While the Governor was disposed to agree with Cobb's proposal, the

General rejected it on several counts. In the first place, heavy guns of the type needed for the operation were unavailable, and there was no assurance that Cobb would be permitted to retain indefinitely the garrison required to hold the town, once it was taken.

From the time Cobb arrived in Quincy until he was reassigned the following September, he never had more than four hundred men on duty along the Apalachicola River. In addition to the river defenses, he had to protect a coastline of approximately one hundred and fifty miles on either side. Hundreds of men were engaged there in boiling sea water in huge kettles and sheet-iron boilers to produce thousands of bushels of salt, a much needed commodity in the Confederacy. Because the salt works were subject to frequent hit-and-run raids by the Federals, Cobb perforce developed the technique of striking lightning blows with small detachments as a means of defense. While his main task was to protect the two most vulnerable points of his district, the Apalachicola River and the three hundred miles of coastline between the Suwannee and Choctawhatchee rivers, he was also expected to cooperate with General Finegan in the defense of East Florida.

It will be recalled that Cobb had drafted and sent to his superiors in Charleston and Richmond a plan to raise a force of some five thousand men to cope with this multiple assignment in Florida. By the time he had returned to his headquarters from his first inspection of river defenses, Beauregard's approval was awaiting him along with an expression of hope that Secretary of War James A. Seddon would act similarly. Early in 1863 Seddon's answer reached Quincy. It was impossible, he explained, to detail men from the area of the main conflict. Cobb could not have the Sixteenth Georgia Regiment transferred to Florida. The law, Seddon pointed out, required that conscripts had to be used to fill up skeleton organizations, but President Davis could suspend this provision upon Cobb's recommendation. In case such action were taken, all arms-bearing persons could be called into service as volunteers

86   HOWELL COBB'S CONFEDERATE CAREER

for special duty for the duration of any local emergency. Afterwards, they would be returned to civilian life and automatically become subject to the conscript laws. Cobb's district, concluded Seddon, was too big to be thoroughly defended; Cobb must be content to rely on small detachments to deter the enemy.

Cobb lost no time in dispatching his views to Seddon. "Do not suspend the conscript law when you call for volunteers," he insisted, "but let the enrolling officer be on hand to take all as will not volunteer. . . ." This was the only way, he warned, to catch every person who should be in the military service. Although Secretary Seddon defended his plan to call up volunteers for short terms, he deferred to Cobb, who announced in late January that he was now authorized to receive companies, battalions, and regiments from the Florida counties between the Suwannee and Choctawhatchee rivers and from twenty-one southwestern Georgia counties. All persons would be accepted, whether or not they were subject to the draft. They were to be mustered in for one or three years, or for the duration of the war. A $50.00 bounty was to be allowed each volunteer and the companies were to be permitted to select their commissioned officers. The announcement explained that those who were willing to serve now had the opportunity of joining volunteer organizations of their own choice. It also warned that men subject to conscription, but who failed to avail themselves of this opportunity, would be summarily enrolled as conscripts.[16]

It is difficult to believe that Cobb could really have expected his plan to work, for while he was preparing it his old friend, William M. Browne, wrote that the Richmond authorities considered conscription a virtual failure

[16] See *ORA*, 1 Series, LIII, 271-273, 276-277; *ibid.*, 1 Series XIV, 230-231, 728-738; *ibid.*, 1 Series, XV, 724; *ibid.*, 1 Series, XXVIII, pt. 2, 190, 214, 272, 451-455; Moreno to Cobb, March 13, May 3, 9, 1863, Clinton Thigpen to Cobb, Dec. 20, 21, 22, 1862, Jan. 3, 1863, H. K. Simmons to Cobb, Dec. 22, Thomas Orman to Cobb, Dec. 18, 20, 22, Citizens to Cobb, Dec. 22, 1862, John J. Guthrie to Cobb, March 30, John D. Atkins to Cobb, Jan. 26, Cobb to his wife, June 10, 19, 26, July 3, 1863, and Cobb's "Announcement," Jan., 1863.

in Georgia, "owing in great measure to the utter imbecility of those appointed to administer it." And, Browne warned on January 21, 1863, unless the situation improved greatly by spring, "our position will be more than critical." Further, he charged that certain "bad designing men in in Crawfordville . . . and elsewhere are doing all they can to bring Joe Brown into open rebellion," and men like Cobb, he concluded, were needed "to counteract their efforts. . . ." In Florida the situation had already deteriorated badly, one functionary writing Cobb that "there is scarcely any part of the state where a single officer can enforce the attendance of conscripts when enrolled." From Alabama he received word that some deserters had vowed not to fight. "I heard one of them swear," wrote his informant, "that if ever he killed a Yanky God dam his soul if it should not be a accident . . . he also wished that there was a million Yankeys in our country. . . ."[17] Cobb conceded to Senator Hunter on March 5 that the conscript law was not working well, but he believed the trouble could be corrected by making conscript officers responsible to department or district commanders.[18]

Almost as pernicious as desertions was the selective feature of the Confederacy's conscription. Under it exemptions were possible for a great variety of occupations. When Cobb reached Florida, he was immediately faced with a virtual stampede by persons seeking to qualify.[19] If he had little discretionary power, he was not lacking in gratuitous advice. Governor Milton, for example, on February 17 strongly advised him against drafting plantation owners and their overseers. While overseers might qualify, the practice of granting them exemptions gave rise to the cry of a "rich man's war and a poor man's fight." According to one of Cobb's friends, Governor Brown, who was running for re-election in 1863, was the most loquaci-

[17] S. Rogers to Cobb, March 12, R. W. Echols to Cobb, March 10, 1863.
[18] In Hunter-Garnett Papers (University of Virginia Library, Charlottesville).
[19] Coulter, *Confederate States of America*, 314-322.

ous promoter of this type of class warfare. He was accused of "preaching agrarian doctrines" to privates for the purpose of inciting them against their officers and the planters. To the latter, it was charged, he persistently referred as "the slaveholders" and "the rich." Although many exemptions came within the letter of the law, some were granted in the most ludicrous manner. An extreme example was that of the French vice-consul in Mobile, who procured one for a native-born Prussian on the grounds that he was a subject of "the fatherland." Such delegation of authority to a foreign official was hardly designed to enhance the Confederacy's prestige. The inept handling of exemptions so demoralized Cobb's own troops that his adjutant reported late in the summer of 1863 that some men were boasting they had never been "rebels" and "never would be" and were urging "reconstruction tomorrow on any terms."[20]

Desertions, exemptions, and uncooperative officials, at both the state and national levels, were not the only obstacles in the way of raising an army to defend Middle Florida. Added to Cobb's woes was a constant pressure for sinecures. Friends, politicians, and relatives all joined to assail the weary General, who over the years had gained a reputation as a dispenser of patronage.

How Cobb was expected to raise an army under these conditions is difficult to imagine. He tried to ameliorate the situation during the winter of 1863 by suspending conscription, joining the order with a warning that all persons liable for service under the suspended act must volunteer or be arrested. The Confederate War Department approved this strange action, announcing that conscription had been suspended in Middle Florida. This effort to coerce volunteering did not soothe ruffled feelings. When the enrolling officers refused to honor the suspension order, confusion was compounded. Little wonder that

[20] Unsigned letter to Cobb, July 1, Pope Barrow to Cobb, June 27, Mrs. Cobb to Cobb, Aug. 7, D. D. McLean to Cobb, May 22, James Barrow to Cobb, Sept. 3, 1863.

within a month of Cobb's departure from Middle Florida, his total force numbered less than thirty-five hundred men. Thus, if the estimate that he began with one thousand is correct, he succeeded in eight months in raising less than twenty-five hundred men. Even so, his was the third largest command in Beauregard's Department of South Carolina, Georgia, and Florida, whose total effectives on August 1, 1863 numbered slightly over twenty-one thousand.[21]

The placing of obstructions in the Apalachicola River to protect the heart of the Military District of Middle Florida was carried to completion immediately after Cobb reached Quincy. A second phase of the defense was the protection of the salt works along the coastline, principally in Taylor County (to the north and west of the Suwannee River), at St. Mark's, and in the St. Andrews Bay area (adjacent to the mouth of the Choctawhatchee River). Cobb also had to be prepared to assist such blockade-runners as were able to reach the ports along three hundred miles of coastline. And he was under orders to assist General Finegan in East Florida.

Except for the presence of the enemy in Apalachicola, there was little activity along the coast until the spring of 1863. Thereafter, Cobb reported the Yankee threat as constant, but he never doubted his ability to deal successfully with it. A few examples illustrate the nature of his problem. One of the first raids came during March at St. Andrews Bay. A small party landed at that point for the purpose of wrecking the salt works, but it was driven off before any damage could be done. A few days later a raiding party captured the C. S. S. *Onward*, a schooner which had slipped through the blockade to Ochlockonee Bay. The raiders set her on fire, rather than see her fall into the hands of Cobb's men. In mid-July the Yankees hit St. Mark's. When Cobb arrived, he discovered that the kettles, boilers, and salt had been destroyed. He spent several days

---

[21] H. Morgan to Cobb, June 8, R. H. Clark to Cobb, June 11, 1863; *ORA*, 1 Series, XXVIII, pt. 2, 249, 272, 482-483.

in the area, changing the location of troops to protect the exposed position of the salt works.

When General Finegan telegraphed Quincy in mid-March that 4,000 Negro troops had landed at Jacksonville, Cobb immediately sent help. Browne promptly wrote that President Davis was pleased with his instant response to the beleaguered Finegan. The Confederate official then proceeded to advise Cobb on how to deal with Negro troops: "I hope if you catch any of our Negro invaders you will instantly hang the white leaders, thrash the Negroes & put them to work, & this without waiting for orders. It is no question for governmental decision. The Negroes after a sound thrashing would cultivate the Cherokee lands to advantage." With the evacuation of Jacksonville late in March, General Lee observed that both Cobb and Finegan "may give us material aid by turning their attention to collecting supplies in Florida and Southern Georgia and forwarding them to the armies at other points. If we do not get this subsistence out of Florida, it will most certainly fall into the hands of the enemy."

If the aid Lee expected from Florida was to be forthcoming, Cobb had need to exercise some supervision over agriculture. The planters of his district, influenced by rumors of an early peace, manifested a strong disposition to plant more cotton and less grain. Against such folly he took a firm stand. Addressing a meeting of planters at Tallahassee in March, he warned that the first responsibility of agriculture was to support the country.   The army must be fed and this could best be done by raising more foodstuffs and less cotton. He later reported that the planters received his exhortations in a cooperative and friendly spirit.[22]

The Confederate authorities seemed pleased with Cobb's work in Florida, despite some rather sharp exchanges that had passed between Quincy and Richmond. These usually

[22] *Ibid.*, 1 Series, XIV, 230-232, 729-731, 751-753, 842; John P. Feller to Cobb, Feb. 25, W. W. Livingston to Cobb, Feb. 25, Browne to Cobb, March 23, Cobb to his wife, Feb. 18 June 5, July 15, 20, 1863; Cobb to his wife, March 13, April 1 1863 (Phillips, 613, 615).

pertained to such matters as procuring arms, the transfer
of the Sixteenth Georgia to Florida, or the approval of
some of Cobb's appointments to commissions. (Early in
May Secretary of War Seddon had refused to approve a
list of Cobb nominations to regimental offices, explaining
that such posts were not yet in existence in Middle Florida.[23]
Seddon may have thought he was balancing his account
with the Georgian by offering him the position of quartermaster general. Cobb promptly turned down the invitation
to go to Richmond, explaining to his wife on May 23 that
". . . it would not only carry me further from home, but
would deprive me of the privilege . . . to take care of my
boys and keep them out of the ranks.")[24]

Brigadier-General Cobb had scarcely settled down in
Florida, when he received word of his brother's death on
December 13 at the Battle of Fredericksburg. "Pa has been
much depressed all day yesterday and today," wrote Howell,
Jr. to his mother on December 17. "It is the severest
misfortune that could have befallen him." To her husband
Mrs. Cobb wrote of Tom's death: "God has done it, it is
right. . . . How ardently had the beloved Tom prayed for
you—how earnestly has he desired to *see* your salvation . . .
I pray that his 'words' may follow him—and that you will
die a converted man."[25] She had long been worried about
his religious views, more than once expressing the hope
that politics would bring him to accept Christianity. When
this failed, she looked to the war as a possible agency of
conversion. While Cobb was in Virginia struggling to get
the Sixteenth in shape, on August 5, 1861 she had written,
"In all your perplexities & annoyances in organizing your
regiment and procuring guns, have you ever asked Divine
assistance?" She implored that he "try it once," assuring

[23] Seddon to Cobb, May 5, 1863.
[24] See Cobb to Seddon, May 14, 1863 (Phillips, 616-617). W. M.
Gardner, Cobb's successor, was to complain that the Middle Florida
staff had been organized "on a strictly family basis" (*ORA*, 1 Series,
XXVIII, pt. 2, 482-483).
[25] Dec. 16, 1863. Cobb seems to have been greatly influenced toward
Unitarianism by Malthus A. Ward, one of his professors at the University of Georgia (see Mrs. Cobb to Cobb, May [?], 1863).

him that such a course would cause his difficulties to vanish. Despite her pleas and his war experiences in Virginia and Maryland, Cobb clung firmly to his unorthodox views. But now there were two deaths, and she hoped they would help break down his resistance. Cobb's mother too was worried about his salvation, but expressed the belief soon after Tom's death that a conversion had occurred. "I wish I could believe it also," wrote the wife to her husband early in 1863. "I want you to come out from among sinners and confess your faith in the Lord," she begged. Only after he had done this could she believe him "safe." She longed to have him "an open and avowed Christian." He must not leave her " 'to tread the wine press alone'." "Let us be one in Spirit," she beseeched, "as we are one in the flesh—and make my last days my best."[26]

Early in 1863 Mrs. Cobb began to show strong feelings of depression. "Day by day," she wrote on February 15, "I carry a weight upon my heart resembling more than anything else a presentiment of evil." The next month Tom, their infant son, died. The mother's grief was overwhelming. She compensated with a deep sense of guilt that lingered for months, confessing repeatedly to her husband that her great sin had been a failure to feel keenly enough her brother's death. God had punished her by taking their infant son. A strong disposition toward withdrawal seized her, doubtless encouraged by Cobb's prolonged absence and his failure to attend their son's funeral. Wondering whether still another punishment awaited her, she complained that life was becoming more difficult and painful. Her future was bleak and horrifying, she stated, and from it she shrank in despair. Her perfect God had made her so imperfect, so much a "sinner." By spring her correspondence suggested that her feelings of frustration drove her to contemplate self-destruction. Her identity with reality was at times extremely vague. She managed to preserve it by intensifying her campaign to get her husband to

[26] Jan. 18, 1863.

accept "Christ and him crucified." "Come—come quickly," she beseeched, "and put it off not too long lest you may be denied the privilege of acknowledging openly your Lord and Master."

Deeply concerned over his wife's distress, Cobb responded to her pleadings with sympathy and understanding. His correspondence reveals him as a man torn between love for his wife and deep convictions about life's ultimate meaning. Habitually contemptuous of authoritarianism and sectarianism, his humanism caused him to extol love, brotherhood, charity, and benevolence. One must achieve these values, he wrote, "to enter upon . . . the higher duties and greater joys in the life to come." Cobb's God was, like the God of such optimistic deists as Franklin and Jefferson, a symbol of man's own powers, those he must try to realize in this life. With its petty wrangles and disputatious sermons, organized Christianity, he believed, defeated the very purpose of life by creating an atmosphere within which the great powers of man were unattainable. Finally, under the constant pressure of his wife's pleading, Cobb conceded that his greatest desire was to be her companion in faith. He was apparently awed by her pious life and may have felt unworthy of the companionship she sought. "Oh how my heart would leap with joy," he wrote, "if I could feel that it was my privelege to . . . take your Christian vows & sit by your side around the communion table. . . ."

During the spring of 1863 he sought the friendship of a Methodist minister of Quincy, whom he called "Mr. Preacher." From him he obtained a copy of *Methodist Pulpit South.* "I could not but feel," he explained, "that in his sight I was not so bad as some think. . . . He is a good man and has won my heart." Meanwhile, Mrs. Cobb's health improved, and her effort to induce Cobb to accept Christianity lost some of its vigor.[27] In consequence, his

[27] During early 1863 Mrs. Cobb and her husband exchanged many letters in which the subject of religion was discussed. For good examples, see her letter of May 4 and his of March 18, May 10, 18, 29, June 14.

religious views came to rest somewhere between his earlier persuasion and that of his wife.

Concern for his wife and his duties as commandant of Middle Florida were not the only claims on General Cobb's time and talents. He had yet another important responsibility—that of watching over his son John, who was managing the numerous family plantations near Macon and Americus. It was while Cobb was in Florida that the plantation became increasingly important as a source of food for the Confederacy. He was now one of the biggest of the Georgia planters. His cotton crop alone netted $30,000, when it was sold early in 1863, and meat and corn were also produced in large quantities. With the Federal blockade tightening, meat and grain became more vital to the war effort than cotton. Early in 1863 Confederate agents appeared at Cobb's plantations, as they did elsewhere, armed with authority to seize meat at the rate of 35¢ per pound. Few understood better than Cobb the new nation's food problems, and he promptly ordered his son to sell. As a result, 22,000 pounds of meat were removed from the Cobb plantations. Thousands of bushels of wheat and corn were also sold during the spring and summer of 1863. The income from these large sales was put to various uses. Operating expenses took a large portion, there were debts to be paid, some was laid aside for taxes, and Cobb, ever the patriot, ordered his son to invest all for which there was no immediate use in 8 per cent Confederate bonds. He preferred to take bonds at par rather than buy them in the market for less, "as I would do nothing to depreciate the value of our currency or credit."

Bringing the Cobb plantations into harmony with the war effort was not a simple task. The inexperienced son John relied almost constantly on his father's judgment. Thus, as the planting season of 1863 approached, Cobb applied to his own acres the advice he had given Florida planters—no cotton. "If want and suffering come upon the country—from planting cotton—the fault shall not be mine," he assured his wife. And so it was with matters of lesser moment. Consequently, the general found it necessary to give his personal attention to buying shoes for slaves, procuring salt to preserve meat, and worrying over the tax bill imposed by the Confederate Congress in April, 1863.[28]

Far more discomposing was the problem of the overseers. Confederate law required payment of $500 a head for their exemption. Cobb had bought exemptions for his overseers during the summer of 1863, only to discover a short time later that Governor Brown had snared four of them for the state military service. Brown, who was running for re-election at this time, was accused of instructing state enrolling officers "to exempt no one especially overseers." Indeed, he was charged with a deliberate attempt to incite a class struggle between rich planters and poor people, and dramatically bidding for the more numerous vote of the one by clubbing the other.[29] Whatever the motive his action put Cobb in an ugly mood. He took his grievance directly to Secretary of War Seddon. He and his three sons were in the army, he declared; he had paid fairly to exempt his overseers, so that his plantations might be cared for in his absence; cotton planting had been abandoned and he was raising only provisions; he had sold generous quantities of meat, wheat, and corn to the government at its price. And now his overseers were to be drafted! "Is this either Law or Justice?" he asked Secretary Seddon on August 19. Delay, he pointed out, would be fatal. "Am I not entitled to as much protection as those who are not in the war?" "Their overseers are detailed and not liable to Gov. Brown's call. I have paid for mine and am in the service—& I ask the same protection. I ask the Government to decide that those overseers of men in the army who have paid the penalty are not liable under the State call to be taken

---

[28] *ORA*, 1 Series, XXV, pt. 2, 737-738; Browne to Cobb, Apr. 29, John A. Cobb to his father, Jan. 21, May 7, 31, to his mother, Feb. 21, March 9, Cobb to his wife, March 16, Aug. 26, and to his son, March 25, Stancel Barwick to Mrs. Cobb, Feb. 11, Mrs. Cobb to Cobb, Aug. 18, 1863.
[29] Cobb to Seddon, Aug. 19, Mrs. Cobb to Cobb, Aug. 7, 1863.

away." On the same day he wrote his wife, "It really
seems there is a complication of troubles & difficulties
gathering around me to annoy & harrass me." And with
a show of philosophical resignation, he added, "We always
suppose . . . our own case to be the hardest & it may be
so with me." But he would not give up the fight to get
his overseers released. If the Secretary of War failed him,
he would carry his case to the courts. (Months later he
was to learn that the courts offered no relief to such
complainants.)[30]

Cobb was to have his lighter moments in Florida, however. Wartime Quincy was a gay place, and the General
and his staff were social favorites. The ladies, of whom
there were numerous widows, entertained with parties and
tableaux, "bringing out some of the gents who were rather
backward before." Charging about on horseback, staff
members and widows doubtless put to flight many an
inhibition.[31] One admirer of the "Brass Buttons" chose
doggerel to express feelings that were surely shared by
many others. Entitled "The Staff," it proudly acclaimed
Cobb and his men as the conquerors of the hearts of
Quincy's fair sex.

That "Eldorado of mismated spouces," as Mrs. Cobb
once called Quincy, set the General's wife to wondering.
Upon learning he was regularly visiting a widow named
Mrs. William E. Kilcrease, she inquired with invidious
reference: "How do you and your nearest neighbor spend
your evenings? You often fall asleep in your own chair—
or on the lounge—while *I am* talking to you. I am curious
to know how *she* keeps you awake—I would like to learn
the gentle art." But there was no hint of unbecoming
behavior. Indeed, she thought it better for his morals that
he associate with some "refined ladies" rather "than altogether with *men*." Recalling her genuine shock at the
grossness of his speech when he once returned from the

[30] Olive H. Shadgett, "Charles Jones Jenkins, J.," in Montgomery
(ed.), *Georgians in Profile*, 235.
[31] John A. Cobb to Lucy Barrow, March 3, 1863.

Peninsula, "all for having only *men* for your associates," on March 1 she warned that upon his return from the "land of flowers," he would be expected "to be very elegant and discourse me entirely in poetry." Cobb parried his wife's chiding thrusts with a light touch. "Don't be surprised," he wrote on the sixth, "if my verse who [*sic*] has slept so quietly from infancy should suddenly rouse up, and give a blast or two." Later, under the pressure of her illness, Mrs. Cobb's tolerance for his aberrations were replaced with a mood of self-pity. When she heard some of the Quincy ladies had ridden with her husband at a military review, she wrote that she understood many were unhappy with Mrs. Kilcrease on account of the marked perference he had shown her. "I felt," she continued, "that I had no form of attraction. Nobody loved *me* any longer."[32]

Far from Quincy and the comparative quiet of Middle Florida a double disaster struck the Confederacy early in July of 1863: Vicksburg fell and Lee's invasion of Pennsylvania was turned back at Gettysburg. The loss of Vicksburg, freeing as it did Federal troops for use elsewhere, instantly placed General Braxton Bragg's Army of Tennessee, then encamped at Chattanooga, in a highly vulnerable position. Late in August authorities in Richmond began to realize Bragg's plight. As commander of the only Confederate force between a rapidly growing Federal army in Tennessee and the rich lands to the Southeast, it was decided to reinforce him from Lee's own troops. Meanwhile Georgians, themselves alarmed by the prospect of a Yankee invasion, began preparations for the defense of their state. To assist in the planning Cobb went to Atlanta early in August. When he returned to Quincy a short time later, he was ordered to serve on a court of inquiry to look into the late Confederate disasters in Mississippi. After some delay the court convened early

[32] June 26, 27, 1863. Mrs. Kilcrease and James Barrow, Cobb's adjutant, were to have been married, but before the ceremony Barrow was killed at the Battle of Olustee (Coulter, *Lost Generation*, 91-94).

in September in Atlanta. With Cobb presiding, the investigation was postponed indefinitely.[33] Before he could leave for Quincy Cobb received orders to remain in Atlanta to organize the militia and other Georgia forces which Governor Brown had ordered there for duty in the Confederate service.[34] A more disagreeable assignment could scarcely have been found for the Brigadier-General. He had no respect for Bragg, for Brown only contempt. Yet, on September 9, 1863 he wrote his good and loyal wife, "I will submit without murmur or complaint."

---

[33] Cobb to David C. Barrow, Aug. 11, 1863 (Barrow Papers); *ORA*, 1 Series, XXVIII, pt. 2, 265; *ibid.*, 1 Series, XXIV, pt. 3, 1045; Cobb to his wife, Sept. 4, 1863.
[34] Atlanta (Ga.) *Confederacy*, Sept. 13, 1863; *ORA*, 4 Series, II, 818; *ibid.*, 1 Series, XXVIII, pt. 2, 348-349.

CHAPTER VI

Commander of the Georgia Guard

BRIGADIER-GENERAL COBB was instructed to organize into battalions, regiments, brigades, and divisions some eight thousand men, largely non-conscripts Governor Brown had offered the Confederacy for local defense. Known at first as the "State Troops" and later as the "Georgia State Guard," this somewhat anomalous agency was destined to be short-lived—it expired early in February, 1864. The men were to be organized into three classes: those who volunteered to serve anywhere in the state; those who offered to serve in a certain district or section of the state; and those who would serve in a town or locality, only. President Davis was anxious that Cobb get the men ready quickly in order to help Bragg defend Georgia against the United States Army, then menacingly poised just north of the Georgia-Tennessee border. However, Cobb was instructed to be careful not to disturb unduly the civilian pursuits of the troops, and he was further ordered to permit the men to elect their own company officers.

Cobb lost no time in tackling his new assignment, reporting to Adjutant-General Samuel Cooper before he had been in Atlanta a week that troops were arriving rapidly, that he expected to complete his work at an early date, and that Governor Brown was cooperating in a most gratifying manner. Two weeks later he again wrote Cooper, noting that about five thousand men had already been organized and that perhaps another five thousand could be raised. Although the Governor's muster rolls carried more than fifteen thousand names, Cobb was convinced that only two-thirds that number were available. He attributed this discrepancy to Brown's inclusion of many conscripts, the infirm, and numerous persons he had arranged to detail to civilian positions.[1]

Although Cobb's initial acts as commander of the Guard had been auspicious enough to win the commendation of Governor Brown, his administrative problems were insuperable. The temporary character of the organization made long-run planning impossible; the territorial rule prevented effective use of the units; belonging as it did to both the state and to the Confederacy, it was torn with conflicts; and maddening confusion soon resulted from the fact that part of the Georgia Guard was to be used in Bragg's and part in Beauregard's department. Moreover, for months there was neither a staff nor a commissary. Of Cobb's command President Davis wrote that it was a "peculiar one," while the Secretary of War considered that the Georgian was not even "at a post." For weeks the puzzled Cobb tried to get the Confederate War Department to rectify some of these incongruities, but Richmond would give him no succor. At length, he sought a way around the odious territorial rule by getting some of the troops to waive it. After deciding this did not go far enough, he divided the state into two districts, separating them by a line from Columbus to Macon, thence through Atlanta to the Chattahoochee River and along its channel to its source. Rome was to become the headquarters of one district, Savannah headquarters of the other.

The game of legal tag which Brown and the Confederate authorities had been playing periodically since the war's inception was resumed about three weeks after Cobb reached Atlanta. At stake was control of the Georgia Guard and this hinged on the procedure to be followed in

---

[1] *Ibid.*, 4 Series, II, 798, 807, 832; Cobb Letter Book, 1863-1864, No. 57 (in University of Georgia Library, Athens, as are also Nos. 55, 56, and 59); John A. Cobb to his wife, Oct. 10, 1863.

selecting officers and commissioning officers elected to fill vacancies. Secretary Seddon and Adjutant-General Cooper were not anxious to renew the Confederacy's quarrel with the Governor, but Cobb, much closer to the problems involved, held some strong views about what should be done. He had no faith in the practice of electing officers, but there was no chance of reversing Davis on this. His principal complaint was directed against Brown's habit of forwarding directly to Richmond the commissions of officers. Cobb addressed himself to Brown, expressing regret that the Governor had seen fit to violate an agreement they had recently reached in President Davis' presence. According to Cobb, Brown had consented to forward to Cobb's headquarters for approval all commissions to fill vacancies. This Brown stoutly denied, informing his adversary that he had not wished to provoke a discussion on the matter and had therefore let it pass with a simple dissent. Cobb countered with the complaint that failure to follow the procedure, which he insisted had been agreed to, was demoralizing the Georgia Guard and rendering discipline impossible. He concluded by promising to submit the entire matter to Richmond, the sort of threat that was unlikely to move Governor Brown.[2]

Richmond's failure to resolve this issue led Cobb to seek an understanding with Colonel H. C. Wayne, adjutant and inspector-general of Georgia. They were close to an agreement based on Cobb's views, but the Governor scotched the attempted rapprochement with the result that procedure in commissioning officers to fill vacancies remained a thorny question throughout the Guard's existence.

The architects of the Georgia Guard had undeniably formed it to assist with the Confederacy's war effort, but they were compelled to fit their organization to the specifications of the Southern political temperament which, preoccupied as it was with a strong sense of personal

[2] Cobb to his wife, Nov. 29, A. R. Lawton to Cobb, Dec. 3, 1863; Candler, III, 421; Cobb Letter Book, 1863-1864, No. 57; *Confederate Union*, Nov. 3, 1863; *ORA*, 4 Series, II, 878.

liberty, placed a premium on the number of effective restraints of governmental action. Therefore, the Georgia Guard could never be wholly the agency of Howell Cobb; always it must bow, as in the case of appointments, to the Governor before it could get on with the work it was ostensibly created to do. Cobb's experience with this military organization reveals how a conscientious and moderately good administrator was to become caught in a highly obfuscating exercise. The Guard must fail, as indeed must the Confederacy, to vindicate that for which its founders were fighting. Success by failure was to burn itself deeply into Southern consciousness.

Still other complications were to confront Cobb. After he had sent 2,500 men into the field, even yet there were no accoutrements, nor was there ammunition. He begged President Davis for 4,000 rifles which the Confederacy had recently purchased from Austria. To remedy the lack of transportation, Cobb, on instructions from his superiors in Richmond, issued an order in late September to seize horses throughout the state. This turned out to be an extremely unpopular move, even Mrs. Cobb ridiculing her husband for threatening her means of locomotion. To feed the 2,500 men, now stationed in Rome, Cobb, still without a commissary, ordered the impressment of all beef in that neighborhood. The problems seemed endless, but Cobb was an astute improvisor.

Stragglers, deserters, and profiteers were not strangers to the disenchanted commander of the Georgia Guard. Earlier in the year he had encountered all of them in Florida. When he came to Georgia to organize the Guard, however, deserters and stragglers were so numerous that he promptly decided to employ three cavalry companies to round them up. In Clarke County and vicinity the cavalrymen were ordered to arm themselves with shotguns. Late in November, with General Bragg's embattled army athwart the Georgia-Tennessee border, Cobb's officers in North Georgia were uncertain whether fighting Yankees was more important than riding herd on deserters.

Despite all of his handicaps, Cobb nevertheless made progress in getting the Georgia Guard ready for duty. Before the end of September Brigadier-General Henry R. Jackson, temporarily in charge of activities in Rome, was preparing to assist the Army of Tennessee. The state of affairs in North Georgia distressed Cobb. On October 8 he wrote his wife that most of the trouble came from the officers' lack of confidence in Bragg. He was pleased that President Davis was soon to visit the Army of Tennessee, and expressed the hope that the Chief Executive, though hostile to General Joseph E. Johnston, would put "Old Joe" in charge.[3]

On October 8 Cobb met the President in Atlanta. In the company of Governor Brown they discussed numerous problems, and, it will be recalled, Cobb supposed an agreement had been reached on the procedure to be followed in forwarding commissions to fill vacancies. The next day Davis and Cobb headed north on the Western and Atlantic Rail Road.[4] What the two men discussed is not known, but it may be assumed that Cobb at least suggested what was wrong with the Army of Tennessee. This was a subject that required exquisite handling by virtue of the President's known fondness for Bragg. The exchanges may have been of such a nature that Cobb felt it unwise to accompany his guest all the way to the front. At any rate, he left the Chief Executive "up the road" and returned to Atlanta.

Although the Georgia Guard was now over a month old, there is no record of its commander having yet seen General Bragg. Realizing the need for a conference with the leader of the army which was to be his unit's principal beneficiary, Cobb planned a meeting for the second week in October, but broken bridges stopped him some ten miles short of his destination. Nevertheless, he visited the troops

---

[3] *Ibid.*, 4 Series, II, 912; Cobb Letter Book, 1863-1864, No. 57; Mrs. Cobb to Cobb, Oct. 7, 1863.
[4] Robert Toombs to his wife, Oct. 9, 1863 (Toombs Papers); Cobb Letter Book, 1863-1864, No. 57; *ORA*, 4 Series, II, 878.

at Rome and learned that many of them were anxious to get back to their farms to gather corn, prepare Chinese sugar cane, and sow wheat. He accommodated them by a generous grant of furloughs and, after returning to Atlanta, reported his action to General Bragg. Later in the month he had to postpone another proposed visit with Bragg, when he received word that Davis was en route to Atlanta, on his way back to Richmond. What transpired between the President and Cobb during the last days of October is unknown, but early the next month, after Cobb finally did get to see Bragg on November 6, he wrote Davis that the commander of the Army of Tennessee now had the confidence of all his subordinates, with the exception of General Longstreet.[5]

Meanwhile, Cobb had to turn his attention to the coast, whence General Beauregard, momentarily expecting an attack on Savannah, had sent a call for troops. Although mortified by another request, Cobb nevertheless complied, transferring Jackson from Rome to Savannah and ordering two regiments of the Guard to report to him. Thus, by the middle of November the Guard was widely dispersed. With headquarters in Atlanta, two of its regiments were now in Savannah and a unit of approximately three thousand men was at Rome, where Brigadier-General Alfred Iverson was in charge. Cobb's primary concern, however, continued to be Bragg's needs, and by mid-November they had become considerable. That a major Federal thrust was in the offing was indicated by the increasing number of raids through the countryside of North Georgia. A favorite target of the raiders was the Western & Atlantic, the main rail connection between Atlanta and the Army of Tennessee. Cobb was determined to keep the road open at all costs. Therefore, he sent Iverson additional cavalry units with instructions to use them in rounding up deserters and stragglers, who were to be put to work protecting the line.

[5] See John A. Cobb to his wife, Oct. 10, 1863. The Cobb to Davis letter is in the Jefferson Davis Papers, Emory University Library, Atlanta, Ga.

Returning from Rome on November 23, Cobb wrote his wife that Bragg was engaged in heavy fighting around Chattanooga. Two days later he warned Iverson of an enemy thrust reported to be aimed at Dalton, Georgia. On the same day Bragg, at the time in serious trouble on Missionary Ridge, wired Atlanta "with great earnestness to send forward the troops now arriving from Alabama— as rapidly as possible." Because of faulty staff work, Cobb had received no dispatches on troop consignments to Atlanta from outside the state and was therefore compelled to rely on such information as he could get from railroad officials. Nevertheless, he was able to send about one thousand men to Bragg, as requested.

Whether the men who were rushed from Atlanta on November 25 arrived in time to share in the Confederate disaster at Missionary Ridge is not known. Having done his best to assist Bragg, however, the commander of the Guard was bitterly disappointed by the sad news from the front. Writing his wife a few days after the battle, he characterized it as the Confederacy's "greatest defeat of the war." It had been a "complete & overwhelming" disaster, he continued, and Georgia was now to become "the great battle ground." "Sulkers & croackers must shoulder their muskets," he warned, and speculators must be brought from their hiding places and "made to disgorge their ill gotten gains—and everybody everywhere must be summoned to the work" of driving the invader from the state. "The work," he assured his wife, "is now begun in Georgia in good earnest."

Bragg wired Cobb two days after the engagement at Missionary Ridge that he had fallen back to Ringgold, Georgia and, although his rear was still under heavy pressure, he would make a stand there. The gloom surrounding Guard headquarters lifted, when news arrived late on November 27 that General Pat Cleburne had on that date given the Yankees "a sound thrashing" at Ringgold. Cobb was much relieved and now wrote, "there is no cause for depondency."

With the main body of the Army of Tennessee at this time near Dalton, its left wing was located in the vicinity of Rome. The Guard, as yet uncommitted to battle, thus composed the army's extreme left. This was roughly the state of military affairs in North Georgia, when Cobb left for the front. Anxious to get an accurate account of recent events, he conferred with General Bragg and Governor Isham Harris of Tennessee. Both assured him that, although the Confederates had been beaten at Missionary Ridge, they had not been overwhelmed.[6] Cleburne's success at Ringgold had given the Army of Tennessee new confidence. Moreover, reports that the Federal army was retiring before Bragg's counterthrust and that its rear was being heavily pounded by General Joseph Wheeler's cavalry gave Cobb new hope as he departed for Atlanta on November 30.

As he reached his headquarters, the Confederate War Department was in the process of transferring Bragg's army to General William J. Hardee. Because Hardee declined to become its permanent commander, a successor had to be found. Hardee's behavior was displeasing to the President, who began the search for another general. Gravely concerned over the army's future, Cobb resolved to have a hand in the selection of its next commander. From Macon, where he had gone to visit his family and celebrate his promotion of December 3 to major-general, he wrote Secretary Seddon that he would leave for Richmond on December 5. Five days later he was in the city as the guest of William M. Browne.

Having come to Richmond principally to get help for his state, which was now in a highly vulnerable situation, the Georgian lost no time in going into action. No one was better equipped to present the case for a reliable commander to lead the Army of Tennessee. He had first-hand knowledge of the military situation back home and few had more friends in important posts in Richmond. To each he

[6] Cobb to his wife, Oct. 17, 28, Nov. 23, 27, 29, 1863; Cobb Letter Book, 1863-1864, No. 57.

emphasized the "absolute necessity" of reinforcing the army and "sending Genl Lee to command it." Impressed with Cobb's earnestness, the President called Lee to Richmond on December 10 for consultation. When the latter indicated a preference for remaining in Virginia, Cobb then recommended the appointment of General Joseph E. Johnston. On the seventeenth he wrote his wife that Johnston would surely get the post as commander of the Army of Tennessee. The next day Johnston was ordered to Dalton, Georgia.[7]

Major-General Howell Cobb was not pleased with what he saw in Richmond in December, 1863. He was most disturbed by the absence of an over-all military policy. For days he conducted a campaign with the civilian authorities to have Lee, Johnston, and Beauregard brought to the capital for the purpose of working out such a policy. If this were done, he believed better relations would ensue between the President and his generals. He was convinced that the Confederacy's strength was being dissipated by the absence of an over-all, high-level military policy. Although Cobb's efforts came to naught, they suggest an insight that was rare among Confederate leaders. Cobb was particularly distressed over the rift between Davis and Congress. This, he wrote his wife on December 17, was "bad—indeed—could not be worse." He observed that "to one less hopeful & sanguine than myself it would cause despondency." Although the Senate was kind enough to extend him the privilege of the floor, he later complained to Vice-President Stephens that Congress, which had once paid him a high tribute, was wanting in "brains."[8]

Early in 1864 Cobb made his first visit to the headquarters of the new commander of the Army of Tennessee.

[7] Stanley F. Horn, *Army of Tennessee* . . . (Indianapolis, 1941), 303-308; Cobb to his wife, Nov. 29, 30, Dec. 10, 17, 1863. Cobb had also gone to Richmond to try to settle his staff problem. For nearly three months he had been administering the Guard almost single handedly. Before he returned, he succeeded in getting Seddon and Davis to approve the transfer of his Florida staff to Atlanta.

[8] *Journal of the Congress*, III, 476; Cobb to Stephens, Jan. 2, 1864 (Phillips, 631).

He found "Old Joe" very congenial and the men of his
army in the best of spirits. Johnston, he wrote his wife on
January 5, would drive the enemy from Georgia and within
six months recover a large part of Tennessee. Quite in
contrast to the delightful visit was his five-miles-per-hour
return to Atlanta on the railroad which was "under the
wise & enlightened management of the *incomparable Joe
Brown.*" It was bad enough to be annoyed by the mis-
management of "this miserable creature, but to think that
honest and good people were still deluded with the idea that
Joe Brown is a marvellously proper man—is to me a
source of *excruciating indignation.*"[9]

Two days before he left Dalton, Cobb wrote an "un-
official" letter to President Davis, outlining in some detail
the plan he had in mind. He believed a strong drive into
Tennessee might conceivably end the war by proving to
the people of the Confederacy, the enemy, and to Europe
the Southern capacity to go on. Moreover, it would replenish the granaries and, unless this were done, the
army could not be fed six months longer. It was more
sensible to recover Tennessee than to strike at Pennsylvania. To invade the enemy's territory would only stir up
his patriotism and strengthen the Lincoln administration
on the eve of the election of 1864. Failure in Pennsylvania
would be followed by the enemy's over-running the Confederacy; failure in Tennessee would not leave the South
so weak that she could not defend herself.[10] Of the one
hundred thousand troops Cobb believed necessary, over
half could be supplied by Johnston and Longstreet. The
remainder might be raised by employing Negroes and re-
pealing the substitute law. If necessary, Beauregard could
supply some fifteen thousand. If more were needed, one
corps could be taken from Virginia. Surely, he asserted
with more boldness than discretion, no one could deny
that Tennessee was more vital to the war effort than Rich-

[9] Cobb to his wife, Jan. 9, 1864. Governor Brown had been re-
elected in late 1863.
[10] Cobb Letter Book, 1863-1864, No. 57.

mond. He concluded by repeating that his plan offered
the only hope of ending what had now become a war of
attrition, a war the South would surely lose, if something
drastic were not immediately done. Davis' reaction to this
interesting proposal is unknown.[11]

Meanwhile, the commander of the Georgia Guard was
sorely distressed at the prospect of losing his own troops.
Enlistments would expire early in February and Congress,
he warned Seddon, could not rely on the state militia for
local defense—the legislature had rendered it independent
of Confederate control. A crisis could be averted only by
authorizing him to recruit from the Guard a new command
for Confederate service. Early in January he requested
Davis and Seddon to arrange for such authorization, im-
ploring the latter to urge Congress to enact a reserve force
bill which Cobb himself had drafted during his latest visit
to Richmond. But Congress was to take its time and, consequently, Davis had to turn down Cobb's request, citing
the legal requirement that all persons of conscript age had
to be assigned to old regiments. Cobb's own military future
was now extremely uncertain. He wrote his wife on January
20 and again ten days later that he would probably have
to return to the field, either in Virginia or at Dalton,
but that he would go, as always, wherever his country
needed him most.[12]

Disappointed by the treatment he had received from
Richmond, Cobb concluded his correspondence on the subject of salvaging the Guard with a "private" letter to
Seddon. He defended his plan by asserting that it would
have assured the Confederacy at least two thousand troops
from Georgia alone. Complaining that Guard personnel
subject to draft would now have to join old army units,
he predicted ruinous results: "They dread the jeers and
sneers which they must encounter from the army more than
they do the bullets of the Yankees and their pride revolts

[11] Cobb to his wife, Feb. 23, 1864.
[12] *ORA*, 4 Series, III, 14, 42. Cobb had urged a reserve force
bill as early as March, 1863. See Cobb to Hunter, March 5, 1863
(Hunter-Garnett Papers).

at the idea of being forced into the ranks under men, their inferiors in every respect save the length of service and experience in the field." Secretary Seddon expressed regret that he had to differ with one for whose judgment he had such great admiration. So highly did he regard the Georgia leader that he submitted all of his letters and telegrams to the President, conceding that "telling him frankly your convictions made me distrust my own." The issue, thought the Secretary of War, had been between "spirited" voluntary organizations and "veteran corps," and the law had left the President no choice.[13]

Thus, on February 4 the Georgia Guard expired. Its men who were liable to conscription were given twenty-day furloughs; the others returned to their homes.[14] Major-General Cobb, now without troops, was for nearly two months unassigned to a military unit. However, within a week General Beauregard wrote that he had requested Adjutant-General Cooper to approve him for the post of commander of the two military districts of Florida. Although pleased, Cobb was far from elated. He had spent enough time, he wrote his wife on February 18 and 23, in the "hard places." His health was again troubling him and he hoped his new assignment would enable him to spend more time with her and their children. As commander of the Guard, he had frequently visited his family in Macon. In fact, Cobb had once entertained the thought of transferring the Guard's headquarters to that city. After one of his numerous visits in early 1864, he had written his wife "that it will take some time to accustom me again to this mode of life." Of the family circle he was growing fonder. After one visit in January, 1864 he eulogized Mrs. Cobb as the ideal wife and mother. "The little ones," he wrote "gathering around your knee—made home and all its association dearer to me than ever."[15]

[13] Cobb Order Book, 1864-1865, No. 56; *ORA*, 4 Series, III, 113.
[14] Inasmuch as the Confederacy never furnished money for the Georgia Guard, its members received no pay for their services (Cobb Letter Book, 1863-1864, No. 55).
[15] *ORA*, 1 Series, XXXV, pt. 1, 581; Cobb to his wife, Jan. 5, 20, 1864.

While Cobb's duties as commander of the Georgia Guard had kept him fairly busy, his political instinct impelled him to maintain his contacts with Richmond and to take the stump now and then in behalf of his country's war efforts. Strangely enough, his ties with the Capitol did not run to Congress, where during the first year of the war he had been the acknowledged leader, but rather they were now, as they had been for over a year, principally with members of the administration. Several interpretations of this unusual relationship may be considered, although none is entirely convincing. In the first place, after leaving Virginia in September, 1862, Cobb had come to rely with increasing confidence upon William M. Browne and Secretary of War Seddon for news and information. Browne had little faith in Congress and Seddon was frequently under sharp attack by some of its members. The correspondence of these men was unlikely to preserve Cobb's earlier fondness for the Confederate legislature. Although he frequently blistered Davis privately, Cobb appears to have come to attribute at least some of the President's aberrations to a Congress which, as he wrote Stephens on January 2, 1864, lacked "brains."[16] This attitude was probably encouraged by the failure of Congress to act promptly on his reserve bill. In this proposal he had taken great pride, believing it absolutely essential to local defense. It is understandable that he should presume to know more about this problem than the lawmakers in Richmond. When they responded with what seemed to be indifference, he was given an opportunity to view the President in linear perspective.

There is also the fact that Congress was coming to be regarded as doing less for the war effort than it might,[17] and Cobb, ever anxious to avoid identification with those who, like Georgia's Governor Brown, were openly at war with Davis, may have believed he could afford no course

[16] Phillips, 631.
[17] For the public attitude toward Congress, see Coulter, *Confederate States of America*, 143-145.

other than outright support of the President. At any
rate, as the fortunes of the Confederacy fell on evil days,
the Georgian's ties with the Chief Executive grew firmer,
and by the same token his opinion of Congress became
more critical. Yet, he felt congressmen to be potentially
useful. Early in 1864 he recommended to Davis that the
"right kind" be encouraged to get out among the people
and make patriotic speeches. He urged Secretary Seddon
to help the President put them on the stump. If such
legislators met enough people, Cobb was convinced the
effect would be a wholesome one. As for himself, he
practiced what he preached. From the time he took over
the Georgia Guard in September, 1863 until two months
after its demise in February, 1864 he found many oppor-
tunities to plead the Confederate cause before public
gatherings in every section of the state. He appeared
before dozens of citizens' meetings, planters' gatherings,
and even the state legislature. With monotonous re-
gularity he denounced extortioners, long a favorite target
with him, and draft dodgers, and on occasion he would aim
an uncomplimentary blast at Governor Brown. Extortioners, he was quoted at least three times as saying, were
not all Jews. "We have many uncircumsised Jews among
us," and he was reported to have recommended that, when
the war was over, "all of them should be circumsised."[18]

With equal vigor he defended Davis. After the suspension of the writ of habeas corpus in February, 1864,
an outcry against the government went up all over Georgia.
Now without a military assignment to worry him, Cobb
sprang to the defense of the President. When some state
legislators and a segment of the Georgia press responded to
Lincoln's announced conditions of peace by inaugurating
what came to be called the Georgia Peace Movement, he
ridiculed the would-be peacemakers. Governor Brown

[18] Cobb to Davis, Jan. 18, 1864 (in Keith Read Collection, University
of Georgia Library, Athens); Cobb Order Book, 1864-1865, No. 56.
For a few of Cobb's speeches, see Augusta (Ga.) *Weekly Chronicle
and Sentinel*, March 23, and *Southern Banner*, Sept. 30, 1863, Jan. 27,
Feb. 10, March 30, 1864.

and Robert Toombs joined the clamor for peace, the latter asserting privately that only the warmongers, whom he claimed were mostly West Pointers, wished to continue the conflict. It would be folly, said Cobb at Newnan late in February, to trust Lincoln. Northern conservatives, with whom the leaders of the abortive peace movement proposed to bargain, had lost their liberty, charged the commander of the late Guard, "by trying to take yours away from you." The people must ever be careful he warned, trusting only in God, themselves, and Jefferson Davis.[19]

Many Georgians thought Cobb's speaking tour of February and March, 1864 and his offer to give the government "all his vast means" were proof of genuine patriotism. Cobb appeared to view his own efforts to stir up public sentiment as a welcome diversion from military duty. To him the campaign was a rewarding one. In its midst he wrote Seddon that he was observing "a perfect renovation in public feeling."[20] Before it was over he was saddened by the death of his young friend James Barrow. Barrow, his former adjutant, who had remained in Florida, had been killed on February 20 at the Battle of Olustee. Cobb's grief was great, and something of his feeling and character is revealed by these simple words, written to the dead man's father: "Except that he was not born to me—Jim was in every other respect my own son."[21]

In the meantime, the War Department, girding itself for the Confederacy's last desperate effort, was busy implementing Cobb's reserve bill, which Congress finally adopted in slightly amended form. Convinced that he would be selected to organize Georgia's new reserve force, the Major-General awaited his new orders from Richmond. In late March, 1864 they reached him—his last and in some re-

[19] *Weekly Chronicle and Sentinel*, Feb. 17, March 9, 17, 23, 1864; clipping in Cobb Folder; Toombs to his wife, March 3, 1864 (Toombs Papers).
[20] *Confederate Union*, Feb. 9, *Southern Banner*, Feb. 17, 1864; Cobb Letter Book, 1864-1865, No. 56.
[21] Coulter, *Lost Generation*, 95; Cobb to Barrow, March 5, 1864 (Barrow Papers).

spects the most rewarding assignment of his entire military career.[22]

---

[22] Cobb to his wife, Feb. 23, 1864; Special Orders, No. 75, March 30, 1864.

CHAPTER VII

Commander of the Georgia Reserve Force

ON APRIL 5, 1864 Major-General Howell Cobb was ordered to Macon to establish headquarters and begin the work of organizing the newly-authorized Georgia Reserve Force. To assist him were Brigadier-General Henry R. Jackson and Colonel Lucius J. Gartrell.[1] Eligible for duty were all able-bodied men between the ages of 17-18 and 45-50, in addition to those on detail from the Provisional Army. They were ordered to rendezvous at the enrolling headquarters in their congressional districts on April 16, and under the supervision of officers to organize themselves into volunteer companies of sixty-four privates and five officers. The men were to elect their own officers, whereupon the companies were to be turned over to the commander of the reserves.

According to Cobb, who had helped draft the legislation creating the units, they were to serve in purely local defense purposes, a "minute man" corps whose members were to be called out to meet emergencies. Otherwise, they were to remain in the workshops and on the farms and to be interfered with as little as possible. Secretary of War Seddon thought it would be wise to procure the higher officers, those above the company level, from the invalid and retired classes. The War Department had agreed to provide quartermasters and surgeons from the Provisional Army. All in the eligible groups were to serve, except

---

[1] Cobb Letter Book, 1864-1865, No. 56; *ORA*, 1 Series, XXXII, pt. 3, 719, 751.

those a medical board declared unfit for field duty. And each commander was to have freedom in selecting men for duty in the various branches of the military service.

From the start Cobb ran into troubles. He had to begin recruiting just as the planting season was getting under way, with the result that many eligibles clamored to tend their farms. He also quickly discovered that some of his first companies could not be released for civilian pursuits because of the increasing necessity of guarding prisoners.[2] Worse still, enrolling officers and medical boards were not always cooperative. Jackson, in Savannah recruiting for Cobb, was disgusted with their corruption and inefficiency, charging they spent most of their time "swindling the government" out of men. Colonel William M. Browne, who spent several months as head of conscription in Georgia, wrote the superintendent of the Bureau of Conscription that enrolling officers were indolent, stupid, apathetic, and corrupt, characteristics he attributed to their low social status.[3]

Nevertheless, Jackson succeeded in recruiting part of a brigade, only to discover that General LaFayette McLaws, assigned to Savannah by Beauregard, was preparing to take his troops and order him to a post in the Department of South Carolina, Georgia, and Florida. Having assigned Jackson to McLaws under orders from the War Department, Cobb was distressed to learn that his second in command was about to be taken from him. He was determined to have the independence of the reserve recognized. Acrimonious missives were exchanged, with Cobb, perhaps mindful of the unkind remarks McLaws had made after the Battle of Crampton's Gap, accusing his old adversary of trying to reduce him to the status of a mere enrolling officer. After months of confusion the difficulty was

[2] Cobb Letter Books, 1864-1865, Nos. 55-56, 59; General Orders No. 28, April 7, 1864 Seddon to Cobb, May 20, 1864; *ORA*, 4 Series, III, 371-372. In June it became possible for men over 50 and boys under 17 to join the Georgia Reserve Force, the latter with their parents' consent.
[3] Jackson to Cobb, May 21, 1864; *ORA*, 4 Series, III, 1049-1050.

finally resolved in Cobb's favor. In July the War Department arranged to have Cobb order Jackson to report with his troops to General Sam Jones, the new commandant of the department, who in turn was to assign him to McLaws for duty in Georgia alone.[4]

The independence of the reserve was also threatened by the Bureau of Conscription. Enrolling officers were not filling up the ranks. To rectify this situation the bureau authorized a supporting force of one cavalry company for each of the state's ten congressional districts. Apparently, the trouble was not corrected by this action, for during the summer President Davis agreed to let his aid, Colonel William M. Browne, go to Georgia on temporary duty to supervise conscription there. Browne, a close friend of Cobb, established headquarters in Augusta. Seeing a chance to get his hands on the cavalry companies, Cobb explained to Browne that, inasmuch as most of the men in them were liable for duty in the Georgia Reserve Force, they should become a part of that organization. He insisted that there were too many independent units in the Confederate service, and this was a good place to begin reducing the number. Months later, as the Confederacy was about to expire, the Conscript Bureau was abolished and its functions were turned over to reserve commanders in the several states.[5]

Except for the threat of invasion, Cobb's most baffling obstacle was still his old adversary, the crafty Governor Brown, one of the few political leaders of his state who understood the implications of the rising tide of popular interest in government that had been unleashed by the Jacksonians. His background identified him with the vocal "wool hat men" of North Georgia. Among them Union sentiment had been comparatively strong before the war, but, like Cobb, Brown had been an ardent Secessionist. To his critics, however, he quickly became a villian; but

[4] Jackson to McLaws, June 27, 1864; *ORA*, 1 Series, XXXV, pt. 2, 572, 589; Cobb Letter Book, 1863-1865, No. 55.
[5] Davis to Cobb, Aug. 11, Browne to Cobb, August 20, 1864; *ORA*, 1 Series, LII, pt. 2, 7-5; *ibid.*, 4 Series, III, 1049-1050; Coulter, *Confederate States of America*, 325.

whatever he was, no one ever denied he was a sharp
politician. He could detect a rousing issue and lay hold of
it with the skill of a master craftsman.

Although Cobb's political career had rested largely on
his ability to adjust to the same forces from which Brown
derived his power, the Major-General labored under the
insuperable handicap of belonging to the substantial ranks
of society. The masses instinctively distrusted him, and
he could not understand why the Governor's persistent
snipping at the heels of Confederate leaders paid off at
the polls. The owner of five plantations, Cobb was never
able to reduce his case to the kind of political symbols
necessary to elicit the emotional response needed for popular support. His excoriations of Yankees, extortioners,
and deserters represented his best efforts in this respect,
but they were not enough. On the other hand, Brown did
more; he invoked the Jacksonian technique of holding before the people an image of terror more frightening than
Cobb's objects of scorn. And that was the image of
scheming leaders in Richmond and their agents, ever bent
on putting something over on the "common man." Years
of experience in county and state election contests made it
easy for Brown to persuade the voters to understand him.
In this respect the Jacksonian tradition played havoc with
the Confederacy. It is one of the ironies of the times that
Cobb, also a Jacksonian of sorts, was to be a conspicuous
victim of the clash of internal social forces within the
Confederacy.

Weeks before Major-General Cobb was appointed to organize the Georgia Reserve Force, Governor Brown was preparing for a renewal of his fight with the Confederate States
of America. He had no intention of undertaking it single-
handedly. In April he submitted to the Georgia legislature
the question of whether the Confederacy was to be permitted to disrupt the state militia by calling into the new
reserve men over 45 and under 18 years of age. Although
Cobb appeared before them in defense of the new corps,
they nevertheless authorized Brown to exempt from duty

all of the state's civil and military officers. Immediately, clerks, deputies, justices of the peace and many other state and local officers were beyond the reach of Cobb's forces. Cobb promptly wrote Brown a long, blistering letter, denouncing his sweeping exemptions and accusing him of passing the responsibility to the legislature. This placed the issue precisely where Brown wished it, and early in May he responded to Cobb's communication by pointing to the legislature's authorization of his action and reminding the Major-General that the state's lawmakers, not the Confederate government, had the right to decide the fate of state employees. Through their legislature the people, he emphasized, had decided to keep a large number of civil officers at home. He must have taken singular delight in revealing to his rival that justices of the peace had the particularly important duty of protecting the people from conscript officers, whom he charged were constantly interfering with the private lives of citizens. The outcry against him, Brown continued, had come from a horde of Confederate officers who were in "comfortable positions in the rear." He claimed this class of "protected" men was more numerous than the "protected state officers." If Cobb was so anxious to fill his reserve, he tauntingly asked, why not refer "to the people the choice of which class was to be withdrawn from their official retreat?" Before the end of May the disputants exchanged at least another brace of recriminatory messages, all replete with personal accusations. On the back of Brown's effort of May 30 the indignant Cobb wrote: "This communication and the author are alike, unworthy of further notice."

Cobb had kept Richmond informed of his quarrel with Governor Brown. In April he warned Adjutant-General Cooper that Brown's sweeping exemptions would seriously interfere with recruitment, sending all pertinent correspondence to the War Department. Upon reading it, Secretary Seddon promptly wrote Cobb that there was no longer any hope of cooperating with the Governor. And this would seem to have been correct, for in July Cobb

informed Davis that Brown had drawn many of his exempts
into the state militia, now 5,000 strong, and turned them
over to General Johnston. The Governor, he continued,
had by this act proved that his original justification for
sweeping exemptions had been a "barefaced falsehood."
Cobb considered taking action to obtain these men for the
"regular Confederate service."[6] However, before he could
act, Brown issued a proclamation, calling into the state
militia all exempts and details of the Confederate government not in actual military service. Cobb immediately
wired Richmond for instructions. On July 16 the Secretary
of War replied by stating that Confederate exempts were
liable for service in the state militia, but that detailed men,
since they had been assigned by Confederate authorities,
were not subject to such service. Perhaps to appease
Brown, Seddon then recommended that Cobb make a "judicious" assignment of details to the militia for temporary
duty. Thinking better of his equivocation, he wired Cobb
five days later that details could be used only by the
Georgia Reserve Force and that, if Brown wished to force
the issue, the responsibility would have to be his. Cobb's
problem was insurmountable, because many of the details,
having received their assignments from Richmond or from
generals of the Confederate Army, were to deny his right
to revoke them.

Organizing the Georgia Reserve amidst the conflicts and
uncertainties which its commander had to face during the
first four months of his incumbency was an onerous responsibility. Yet Cobb was able to report progress. By
June, a little over two months after his appointment, he
had four regiments (approximately seven hundred and
fifty men) at Andersonville, a battalion of six companies
at Macon, two companies at Augusta, and six companies
at Savannah. He predicted a total of eight regiments of
this type to guard prisoners and public works, though
Brown's sweeping exemptions were to make this goal diffi-

6 Cobb Letter Books, 1863-1865, Nos. 55-56; Candler, III, 515-527,
573; ORA, 4 Series, III, 530-531.

cult to attain. In addition to this type of continuous-duty
unit, he planned to organize Confederate details into companies and battalions of "minute men" for local defense.[7]
The law clearly entitled Cobb to such use of the details and,
when Brown threatened to seize them, the Major-General
had no choice but to resist as subbornly as he knew how.

Late in July relations between Brown and Cobb suddenly
took a turn for the better. On the twenty-ninth the Governor appeared in Macon and informed the General that he
would be at the latter's headquarters in the afternoon. In
striking contrast to his late behavior, Brown assured his
rival that he would be glad to see him and to cooperate in
the defense of Milledgeville and Macon. The enemy was
coming, and, for the moment at least, both men showed a
strong disposition to fight only Yankees.

Military movements north of Atlanta had been a matter
of grave concern to Cobb ever since his return from Florida
in the fall of 1863. As commander of the Georgia Guard,
he had been closely identified with them. One month after
he assumed his duties with the Georgia Reserve Force,
General W. T. Sherman began his drive toward Atlanta.
In June Cobb visited General Johnston's headquarters and
saw at close range the desperate situation confronting the
Army of Tennessee. Two weeks later he implored Seddon
to turn General Nathan Bedford Forrest loose on Sherman's lines and reiterated his confidence in Johnston. He
marveled at "Old Joe's" ability to fall back with everything
except the countryside, "which he could not take with him."[8]

By this time Atlanta citizens were reported in "terrible
panic," and Mrs. Cobb, now in Athens, feared her friends
and neighbors were likely to become similarly beset. On

---

[7] Candler, III, 591. It is difficult to follow the Confederate government's application of the rules on exemptions and details. However,
they were treated as distinct groups, "exempts" being those temporarily excused from service and "details" those in the service who
had been assigned to specific duties considered essential to the war
effort. Seddon to Cobb, July 16, 21; L. J. Gartrell to Cobb, May 21,
1864; Cobb Letter Book, 1863-1865, No. 55; *ORA*, 1 Series, XXXIX,
pt. 2, 801.

[8] Brown to Cobb, July 29, Cobb to his wife, June 14, July 4, 29, Mrs.
Cobb to Cobb, July 11, 1864; *ORA*, 1 Series, XXXVIII, pt. 5, 858.

July 12 L. J. Gartrell notified Cobb that he was ready to
move Georgia Reserve Force stores and wagons out of the
city at a moment's notice. In mid-July, however, Cobb was
still confident Atlanta would not fall; but when Johnston
was relieved a few days later and the enemy now literally at
the city's gate, he became apprehensive. He assured his
wife that she and her neighbors would be spared, because
Johnston, now Cobb's guest in Macon, had, before turning
the Army of Tennessee over to General John B. Hood,
instructed General Joseph Wheeler to strike Sherman's
rear in case the Federals attempted a raid on Athens.[9]

Federal raids in the direction of Macon increased as
Sherman drew closer to Atlanta. Of particular concern was
General George Stoneman's raiders. They had been ordered
to skirt General Hood's right and tear up the tracks of the
Central of Georgia Rail Road, seize Macon, and head for
Andersonville to release prisoners there. Robbing and
burning indiscriminately along the way, Stoneman's party
reached the Ocmulgee River, opposite Macon, on July 30.
Before they could cross, the raiders were met by a force of
Georgia Reserves, state milita, and residents, all commanded
by Cobb. Present during this action—known as the Battle
of East Macon—were Brown, who obligingly turned his
troops over to Cobb, and Johnston, to whom Cobb politely
offered the command. Repulsed, the raiders turned and
raced off only to run into General Iverson's cavalry force,
which captured Stoneman and some six hundred of his
men.[10]

Cobb was cheered by the outcome of his brisk encounter
with Stoneman. He was particularly grateful to Johnston,
of whom he wrote: "He showed himself not only the
General but the gentleman that I had always believed him
to be." Of the Georgian, Johnston stated that "by his own
courage and judicious disposition" he assured victory. The
most generous acclaim was accorded Brown by his organ,

    [9] Cobb to his wife, July 16, 20, 22, 1864, (Phillips, 648).
    [10] *Southern Banner*, Aug. 10, 1864; *ORA*, 1 Series, XXXVIII, pt. 3,
688-696; Cobb to his wife, Aug. 3, 1864; "Official Report of the
Battle of East Macon."

the Atlanta *Intelligencer,* which reported that Cobb and Johnston "were on the field" observing Brown lead the troops. Cobb conceded that the Governor had done his duty—he had done nothing more than turn over the state troops which by accident happened to be present when hostilities began.[11]

The inglorious fate of Stoneman did not put an end to Federal raids south of Atlanta, however. On September 1 communications between Atlanta and Macon were cut at Jonesboro. Hood, now virtually isolated, gave up the former city and fell back to Lovejoy's, a short distance south of Jonesboro, where he joined Hardee's corps. In the meantime, Sherman put out peace feelers to Georgia's Governor Brown. Richmond now bestirred itself, Seddon ordering Brown on August 30 to turn over his 10,000 state troops to Confederate officers. Two days later the President urged Cobb to go to Hardee's aid, specifically ordering him to cut the enemy's supply lines. Whether enrolled or not, decreed Davis, every man who could fight "should now be put into requisition."[12]

Thoroughly disturbed by events in Georgia, Davis decided to go to Macon to talk with Cobb and to visit the front. On September 24 he arrived at the Georgia Reserve Force headquarters. Cobb introduced him to a crowd at the Baptist church and the President made a speech. He urged the people to unite and crush the invader, made some unkind references to Joe Johnston, and then asserted that, "if one half of the men now absent without leave will return to duty, we can defeat the enemy."[13] His indiscreet remarks did not go unnoticed; the Charleston *Mercury* hoped it would soon be able to deny their authenticity and the Augusta *Weekly Chronicle and Sentinel* charged that

[11] Cobb to his wife, Aug. 3, 1864; Joseph E. Johnston, *Narrative of Military Operations* . . . (New York, 1874), 369-370; Cobb Letter Book, 1863-1865, No. 55.
[12] "Correspondence Between Secretary of War and Governor Brown," 3 (in University of Georgia Library, Athens); *ORA*, 1 Series, XXXIX, pt. 2, 811.
[13] John A. Cobb to his wife, Sept. 26, 1864.

the President was yielding to personal prejudice and acrimony.[14]

From Macon the President and Cobb went to Palmetto, about twenty-five miles west of Lovejoy's, where Hood had taken his army on September 21. They visited with him and Governor Isham Harris of Tennessee for three days, each making speeches to the troops. It was probably at this time that the decision was made to add to Cobb's duties those of a new command to be known as the District of Georgia, embracing the posts of Macon, Columbus, and Augusta. The Major-General was to be responsible to the Army of Tennessee. On September 28 Cobb was officially assigned to his additional duties. After returning to Macon, Davis and Cobb then went to Augusta. There on October 2 they met Beauregard and Hardee. Again the President and his generals delivered speeches and decided two command problems:[15] Beauregard was to take over the new "Military Division of the West" and Hardee was to go to Charleston as head of the Department of South Carolina, Georgia, and Florida.[16]

By mid-October the reformed commands were at work, both Hood and Beauregard having ordered Cobb to move on to Atlanta as soon as possible with all the troops he could collect. To assure a sizeable striking force, the state militia under Major-General Gustavus W. Smith was taken over by Cobb, who promised absentees all would be forgiven, if they voluntarily came forward. By November 1 Cobb and Smith had moved their army of approximately seventeen thousand reserves and militiamen to "Camp Bald Head" near Lovejoy's. Here they began repairing the railroad to Atlanta in preparation for a demonstration against that city which had been in enemy hands since early September.

For nearly two weeks Cobb and Smith waited at Lovejoy's, receiving conjectures and indecisive reports on Sherman. Then, on November 11 Hood sent Cobb an ominous order to tear up the tracks in "front" of Sherman. Portentous indeed were Beauregard's directives three days later that Cobb immediately complete the defenses of Macon and make no further effort to reconstruct the railroad to Atlanta. On the fifteenth Sherman set fire to the city he had held for more than two months and divided his army, sending the left wing to Sandersville by way of Milledgeville, and the right by way of Jonesboro with orders to simulate an attack on Macon. The next day the right wing cavalry leader, Brigadier-General Judson Kilpatrick, reported that Cobb and his army were strongly posted at Lovejoy's. Actually, Cobb and Smith had begun falling back on the fifteenth and two days later they were in Macon. Cobb now assured Davis that the Yankee juggernaut was bound for that city and urged the President to order a concentration of power at Charleston, Savannah, and Wilmington. Inasmuch as Sherman had abandoned his own lines and was literally adrift in the land of the enemy, such a concentration of Confederate power could be used to destroy him and this, insisted the Georgian, "would be the greatest result of the war." Otherwise, Sherman would march blithely on to Savannah and Charleston.[17] Whatever else may be said of Cobb's proposal, it had at least the merit of pointing up the Confederacy's persistent bungling of the strategy problem. By dispersing its forces over a vast terrain that was rapidly becoming trackless, the South had weakened its chance of making effective warfare at any single point. It will be recalled that Cobb had urged, when in Richmond about twelve months earlier, that Davis and his generals design an over-all plan for conducting the war. He had also proposed a major spring offensive against the Federal forces in

[17] Summarized from *ORA*, 1 Series, XXXIX, pt. 3, 821, 911; *ibid.*, 1 Series, XLIV, 54, 362-367, 861-863, 931-933; Beauregard to Cobb, Oct. 16, to M. L. Smith, Nov. 14, 1864; Cobb to his wife, Nov. 3, 1864 (Phillips 655-656); John A. Cobb to his wife, Nov. 3, 1864; Cobb Letter Book, 1863-1865, No. 55.

Tennessee. Cobb had strongly defended both recommendations, and although Davis had tried to get Johnston to take the offensive early in 1864, neither of the Georgian's recommendations was adopted. However, they suggest the kind of imagination, insight, and boldness usually attributed to successful military planners.

The best Davis could do in response to Cobb's latest plea for help was to exhort him, on November 18, "to get out every man who can render any service . . . and employ Negroes in destroying roads. . . ." He agreed the task was difficult and expressed the hope that Hardee and General Richard Taylor would soon be on hand to help. Cobb would of course realize, continued the Chief Executive, "the necessity for the greatest exertion."

In the meantime, Beauregard prepared for a concentration at Macon by urging Hood, Taylor, and Hardee to give Cobb all the men they could spare. Taylor and Hardee were ordered there in person, and Beauregard was soon to be on his way. Hardee arrived on November 19 and promptly took command. By this time Cobb had divined that the enemy was simply planning a feint at Macon, although he wrote his wife, November 19, that he expected a small brush. He had indeed exerted himself during the past week, reporting little sleep for four nights and admitting that he felt "quite stupid."

The brush Cobb had predicted turned out to be two separate engagements. On the day Hardee arrived, Kilpatrick struck Wheeler's cavalry at East Macon and for several days thereafter was busy tearing up the tracks on the Macon-Milledgeville Rail Road. On the twenty-second Wheeler attempted to drive him off by attacking at Griswold Station, about four miles east of Macon. Brisk action followed, "the saber being principally used." Although Wheeler managed to take a few prisoners, he was badly used up, losing, according to Cobb, some five hundred men, killed and wounded. Thus did Sherman roll on, past Macon toward Milledgeville and thence to Savannah. Storming through Baldwin County, the Yankees wrecked one of Cobb's own plantations.[18]

From Franklin, Tennessee came news of the ill fortune that had befallen Hood's army in mid-December. A few days before Christmas Sherman occupied Savannah. Before the year's end Cobb addressed another appeal to the President, this time opining that Hood's disaster had depressed the people more than Sherman's march. For the President's edification he sought to penetrate the tantalizing mystery of Sherman's intention by predicting, on December 28, that the Union commander would retrace his steps to middle Georgia and then strike at "our granary," as the southwestern part of the state had come to be called.[19]

Altogether, Major-General Cobb was alarmed at how completely the agonizing events of late 1864 had stupefied the public. If the Confederacy were to survive, he was convinced that the state of public opinion must be speedily altered. Thus, on January 6, 1865 he wrote Davis again, "a monstrous plain letter." "It is useless," he asserted, "to disguise the fact that there is a deep despondency in the public mind—extending in too many instances to disaffection." He admitted to "deep mortification" upon learning the names of some who had attended submission meetings in Savannah. Things were no better in other seaboard counties, in Southwest Georgia, and elsewhere. On the other hand, he assured Davis that there was a true and loyal sentiment, which, though disaster-ridden, had borne up well, and would yet become the prevailing sentiment, if properly encouraged. "You can well understand," he continued, "that the teachings of those who are hostile to the Administration has prepared the way for all this despondence and disaffection to be concentrated in a feeling of opposition to your Administration and discontent with the Confederate Government." Without mentioning

[18] *ORA*, 1 Series, XLIV, 362-367, 406, 866; Cobb to his wife, Nov. 24, 1864; Lucy B. Cobb to Bessie(?), Nov. 28, 1864 (Barrow Papers).
[19] In Davis Collection (Emory University, Atlanta).

names, he asserted that some of those who had raised the
whirlwind "would now cellar it." Their influence could
do much good, if properly directed. For the Confederacy's
chronic ailment he confessed he was without a remedy.
However, the President must treat the symptoms. First,
Hood must go—people no longer had faith in him. To hold
on to him longer encouraged public distrust. Next, Joe
Johnston must be restored—in him people had confidence.
Further, the volunteer principle of keeping up the army
must be adopted. It would, he promised, dispel gloom and
despondency. He was sure the President understood that
the present state of feeling and the admittedly odious conscript law would make it difficult for enrolling officers
"to add recruits to your army—or return to their commands
deserters and absentees." In concluding this "monstrous
plain letter," Cobb repeated his fear that Sherman would
yet carry out his threat to devastate Southwest Georgia.
Help must be sent at once—if not from Beauregard, then
from elsewhere.[20] Cobb's concern over that section of his
state was well-founded. His wife and the children had
gone there (to Americus), having left Macon as Sherman's
threatened invasion grew more ominous.[21] As a principal
source of food, the region's importance had long been
appreciated. Because of its large Negro population, Cobb
had frequently asked for troops to guard it against possible
uprisings. Now, more directly connected with the war's
military movements was the big, highly-publicized Sumter
Prison, at Andersonville, for which the Georgia Reserve
Force was responsible.[22] But Richmond did not share
Cobb's concern over Southwest Georgia. Far more disturbed
over the vulnerable position of Augusta, early in January
the War Department ordered Cobb to move his head-

[20] In Cobb Letters (Duke University Library, Durham, N. C.); see
also Cobb to his wife, Jan. 23, 1865.
[21] Cobb to his wife, Jan. 24, 1864.
[22] Cobb had notified Richmond of the inadequacies at Andersonville,
advising construction of another prison camp at Union Springs, Ala.
However, as additional captives arrived, he did the best possible to
accommodate them. See Cobb Letter Book, 1863-1865, No. 55;
Special Order No. 98, Apr. 24, 1864.

quarters to that city "with all practicable dispatch."[23] The prospect of a tour of duty in Augusta greatly displeased him, however, and he promptly forwarded a lengthy protest to Cooper. He complained that the new assignment would take him too far from the "Granary of the Confederacy," and because Beauregard had recently put Augusta in Hardee's department, it would also place him in the anomalous position of having his headquarters outside his district. Arriving at his new station on January 18, Cobb confided to his wife on the following day that many Augustans were disloyal and their homes would have to be abandoned, as there were not enough troops to "make a respectable picket line around the city." Lamenting that he had nothing to do at his new headquarters, he declared that either he or General Hill, the officer in charge of Augusta, would soon be ordered elsewhere. He confidently expected to be recalled to Macon. And sure enough, on January 31 he was back at his old headquarters.[24]

During Cobb's brief interlude away from Macon the War Department had sent Brigadier-General W. T. Wofford to North Georgia as the head of an independent command to round up deserters and absentees. Upon returning to Macon, Cobb immediately addressed a sharp note to Adjutant-General Cooper, deploring the rise within his district of such independent commands and demanding a clarification of his position as "commander" of the Military District of Georgia. His peremptory plea unheeded, Cobb turned to his friend, General Joe Johnston, lately recalled to the Army of Tennessee, but it was not until late in March that Johnston finally resolved the difficulty by placing the Georgian in charge of the Department of Tennessee and Georgia. This was Hood's old post and as its commanding officer Cobb was entitled to Wofford's troops.[25]

[23] *ORA*, 1 Series, XLVII, pt. 2, 1005.
[24] Cobb to Cooper, Jan. 16, 1865 (Cobb Letters) ; Cobb to Mrs. C. C. Clay, Jan. 21, 1865 (in Clement C. Clay Papers, Duke University Library, Durham, N. C.) ; Cobb to his wife, Jan. 31, 1865 (Phillips, 659).
[25] Cobb Letter Books, 1863-1865, Nos. 55, 59; Special Orders, No. 12, March 27, 1865. Middle and West Georgia were in this command.

The problem of defending Southwest Georgia acquired a new dimension shortly after Cobb's return to Macon. Federal troops were now driving eastward across Alabama. Cobb must prepare at once to turn them back at the Chattahoochee River.   But in Georgia the sinews of war had grown exceedingly feeble.   In nearly every part of the state deserters were organized into predatory bands that were committing outrages against helpless citizens.   When confronted with the impotent enrolling officers, now in the reserve, these organized outlaws were often defiant.   In one county the local police prevented the enrolling officer from arresting deserters; in another two hundred cavalrymen, ordered to round them up, were ambushed and cut to pieces.   To escape the wrath of these outlaws and bushwhackers, helpless citizens often accorded them shelter. Others were victimized, some complaining that nothing was being done to protect them from marauders.   On at least one occasion Cobb personally arranged to consult with local citizens on a method of dealing with this problem; but it was now too late to stem the tide of popular resentment.   Many people yearned for the order and stability they believed only peace would bring.   Peace meetings thus took such a hold of the popular imagination that Cobb admitted to President Davis in late January that nearly all wished the war to end.[26]   On March 8 the Augusta *Chronicle,* one of the state's leading newspapers, asserted that nine-tenths of the citizens of Madison and adjoining counties favored the calling of a state convention to arrange for peace.

Although Cobb realized that many Georgians had lost the will to resist, he nonetheless dutifully proceeded with preparations to prevent the invader from crossing the Chattahoochee River.   But at this very moment he was

Hill commanded the remainder of Georgia, which was attached to the Department of South Carolina, Georgia, and Florida (*ORA,* 1 Series, XLVII, pt. 3, 700).

[26] B. F. White to Lamar Cobb, Jan. 6, T. T. Dorough to Cobb, March 11, Duncan L. Clinch to Cobb, April 4; *Southern Banner,* Feb. 15, 1865; Cobb Letter Book, 1865, No. 59; *ORA,* 1 Series, LIII, 393-394.

again to be caught in the fatal web of divided purpose. In late March, just as he was preparing to concentrate his meager forces against the threat from Alabama, Cobb received a telegram from General Robert E. Lee, directing him "to prepare for an important movement in North Georgia." A week later he was making plans to place Wofford's 3,000 men at Lee's disposal. Simultaneously, he received assurance that two regiments of state troops would be supplied for the "movement." With Federal troops now racing for the Chattahoochee, Johnston, acting under instructions from the President, ordered Cobb on April 8 to take his men into Alabama. This sort of divided purpose was to see the Confederacy through to the bitter end.[27]

Before leaving for Montgomery to confer with the Governor of Alabama, Cobb made one more appeal to Davis, asking him to send help to save the crops of Southwest Georgia and the arsenals east of the Mississippi. These, the Chief Executive was reminded, were "essential to our success," and with the touch of a comforter Cobb added, "true men are bold, defiant and hopeful." For a change the harassed Georgian had a stroke of good luck. Governor Brown gave him permission to take the militia across the state line. This was the situation as he left for Montgomery on April 9 or 10. There it was decided to put him in charge of the defenses east of that city.[28]

Columbus, Georgia became the local point of Cobb's defense plan. There he gathered what forces he could, but to little avail, for on April 17 the city fell to Major-General J. H. Wilson, Cobb escaping "in the dark," with about six hundred men. Upon his arrival in Macon, he received a dispatch from Beauregard, dated April 20, announcing an armistice. Embattled hosts everywhere were to cease fir-

[27] Cobb to Norman Smith, March 25, April 1, 1865 (in C. C. Jones, comp., *Confederate States of America Constitution, Autograph Letters, and Portraits* . . . , n.p., n.d., Nos. 20, 49); Wayne to Cobb, April 1, 1865; Cobb Letter Book, 1865, No. 59; *ORA*, 1 Series, XLVII, pt. 3, 767.
[28] Cobb Letter Book, 1865, No. 59; Endorsement on Cobb to Brown, April 9, 1865 (Cobb Letters); *ORA*, 1 Series, XLIX, pt. 2, 1239.

ing and hold their positions for forty-eight hours. Thereupon, Cobb sent a flag of truce to Wilson. Fourteen miles west of the city the flag party prepared to meet the advance units of Wilson's command, which, instead of receiving Cobb's emmisaries, raced on into Macon and demanded its unconditional surrender. The end had come for Cobb. He gave up under protest, justifiably claiming a violation of the truce.

After the surrender Cobb's behavior was described by Wilson as exemplary. But the defeated General made it abundantly clear that he had been an original Secessionist. He was careful to point out that he had not followed his state out of the Union, but rather it had followed him. About a month after the surrender he was arrested, and then paroled by President Andrew Johnson while en route to prison.[29]

In the fall of 1865 Cobb and James Jackson opened a law office in Macon. In a short while they were making money. Cobb's plantation also began to provide an income. Long in politics, he was soon to express himself freely on the major public issues of the immediate post-war era. As did many Southerners, he deeply resented Reconstruction. Of Negroes he wrote some months after the war that they had behaved generally "better than we had a right to expect." They were, he thought, not "by nature vicious," but "constitutionally lazy—and it is from that cause that we are to look for the most of our troubles in dealing with them in the future."[30]

On September 7, 1868 Cobb wrote his wife: "Today I enter my fifty fourth year, a tolerable old man who has reached the summit of life's journey—and must soon begin its descent."

A little more than a month later, on October 9, he dropped dead in the lobby of New York's Fifth Avenue

[29] B. D. Fry to Cobb, April 14, Cobb to Beauregard, April 20, to Wofford, April 21, 1865; *ORA*, 1 Series, XLIX, pt. 1, 254-370, pt. 2, 383; 783-787, 901-922; *ibid.*, XLVII, pt. 3, 814.
[30] Cobb to his wife, Nov. 2, 24, to Richard Taylor, Dec. 8, 1865.

Hotel, as he and his wife and their eldest daughter were talking with friends. They had been on a holiday to Saratoga and were on their return to Georgia. The body was sent to Savannah by steamer and thence to Athens by railroad. There he was buried on October 15. The editor of the *Southern Watchman,* who had opposed the Major-General's policies and politics for years, described the funeral services as the "most impressive ceremony ever witnessed in our town.[31]

[31] Oct. 21, 1868.

Bibliography

Manuscripts

The Barrow Papers, Howell Cobb Letter Books, Cobb Order Book, Cobb Folder, T. R. R. Cobb Letters, Erwin Collection, Florence H. Heidler Collection, Lamar Family History File, Keith Read Collection, and the Robert Toombs Papers are in the University of Georgia Library, Athens. The Pierre G. T. Beauregard Papers, Clement C. Clay Papers, and the Howell Cobb Letters are in the Duke University Library, Durham. The Jefferson Davis Papers and the Alexander H. Stephens Papers are in the Emory University Library, Atlanta, Ga. The Hunter-Garnett Papers are in the University of Virginia Library, Charlottesville. The Jackson-Prince Papers, the LaFayette McLaws Papers, and the William P. Miles Papers are in the University of North Carolina Library, Chapel Hill. The Howell Cobb Collection is owned by Mr. Will Erwin, Athens, Ga.

Sellers, Ruby L. "The Civil War Career of Howell Cobb." Unpublished Master's thesis, University of Georgia, Athens, 1947.

Books and Articles

Acts and Resolutions of the Second Session of the Provisional Congress of the Confederate States. Montgomery, 1861.

Boykin, Samuel, ed. *A Memorial Volume of the Hon. Howell Cobb of Georgia.* Philadelphia, 1870.

Brooks, Robert P. "Howell Cobb and the Crisis of 1850," *Mississippi Valley Historical Review,* IV, 279-298 (Dec. 1917).

————, ed. "Howell Cobb Papers," *Georgia Historical Quarterly*, V-VI, *passim* (Sept.-Dec., 1922).

Bryan, T. Conn. *Confederate Georgia*, Athens, 1953.

Candler, Allen D., ed. *Confederate Records of the State of Georgia*. Atlanta, 1909-1910. 6 vols.

Cobb, Howell. "Necessity for Party Organization," *Congressional Globe*, 30 Cong., 1 Sess., 775-779 (July 1, 1848).

Cobb, John A. "Civil War Incidents in Macon," *Georgia Historical Quarterly*, VII, 282-284 (Sept., 1923).

Correspondence Between Governor Brown and the Secretary of War, Upon the Right of the Georgia Volunteers, in Confederate Service, to Elect Their Own Officers. Milledgeville, 1863.

Correspondence Between the Secretary of War and Governor Brown, Growing Out of a Requisition Made Upon the Governor for the Reserve Militia of Georgia To Be Turned Over to Confederate Control. Milledgeville, 1865.

Coulter, E. Merton. *The Confederate States of America, 1861-1865*. Baton Rouge, 1950.

————. *Lost Generation: The Life and Death of James Barrow, C. S. A.* (Confederate Centennial Studies, No. 1). Tuscaloosa, 1956.

Fielder, Herbert. *A Sketch of the Life and Times and Speeches of Joseph E. Brown.* Springfield, 1883.

Freeman, Douglas Southall. *Lee's Lieutenants: A Study in Command.* New York, 1942-1944. 3 vols.

Hassler, Warren W., Jr. *General George B. McClellan: Shield of the Union.* Baton Rouge, 1957.

Hesseltine, William B. *Civil War Prisons: A Study in War Psychology.* Columbus, 1930.

Hill, Louise B. *Joseph E. Brown and the Confederacy.* Chapel Hill, 1939.

Horn, Stanley F. *The Army of Tennessee: A Military History.* Indianapolis, 1941.

"Howell Cobb of Georgia," *United States Magazine, and Democratic Review,* XXV, 266-276 (Sept., 1849).

Hull, A. L., ed. "The Correspondence of Thomas Reade Rootes Cobb, 1860-1862," *Publications of the Southern Historical Association,* XI, 147-185 (May, 1907).

Johnston, Joseph E. *Narrative of Military Operations, Directed, During the Late War Between the States.* New York, 1874.

Johnson, Robert U. and Clarence C. Buel, eds. *Battles and Leaders of the Civil War. . . .* New York, 1884-1887. 4 vols.

Johnson, Zachary Taylor. *The Political Policies of Howell Cobb.* Nashville, 1929.

Jones, C. C., comp. *Confederate States of America Constitution, Autograph Letters, and Portraits of the Signers Constitution of the Confederate States.* N.p., n.d.

Journal of the Congress of the Confederate States of America, 1861-1865. Washington, 1904-1905. 7 vols.

Journal of the Proceedings of the House of Representatives of the General Assembly of the State of Florida. Tallahassee, 1863.

Journal of the Public and Secret Proceedings of the Convention of the People of Georgia, Held in Milledgeville and Savannah, 1861. Together with the Ordinances Adopted. Milledgeville, 1861.

Lonn, Ella. *Salt as a Factor in the Confederacy.* New York, 1933.

McClellan, George B. *McClellan's Own Story.* New York, 1887.

Matthews, James M., ed. *The Statutes at Large of the Provisional Government of the Confederate States of America, from ... February 8, 1861, to ... February 18, 1862. ...* Richmond, 1864.

Mays, Elizabeth, " 'The Celebrated Mrs. Cobb'—Mrs. Howell Cobb," *Georgia Historical Quarterly,* XXIV, 101-122 (June, 1940).

Montgomery, Horace. *Cracker Parties.* Baton Rouge, 1950.

———, ed. *Georgians in Profile: Historical Essays in Honor of Ellis Merton Coulter.* Athens, 1958.

Moore, Frank, ed. *The Rebellion Record: A Diary of American Events, with Documents, Narratives, Illustrative Incidents, Poetry, etc.* New York, 1861-1868. 11 vols. and sup.

Official Reports of Battles. Published by Order of Congress. Richmond, 1862.

Owsley, Frank L. *King Cotton Diplomacy.* Chicago, 1931.

Phillips, Ulrich B., ed. *The Correspondence of Robert Toombs, Alexander H. Stephens, and Howell Cobb.* Washington, 1913.

Provisional and Permanent Constitutions, Together with the Acts and Resolutions of the First Session of the Provisional Congress, of the Confederate States. Montgomery, 1861.

Reports of the Operations of the Army of Northern Virginia, from June, 1862, to and Including the Battle at Fredericksburg, Dec. 13, 1862. Richmond, 1864. 2 vols.

Richardson, James D., comp. *A Compilation of the Messages and Papers of the Confederacy.* Nashville, 1905. 2 vols.

Sargent, Nathan. *Public Men and Events from the Commencement of Mr. Monroe's Administration, in 1817, to the Close of Mr. Fillmore's Administration, in 1853.* Philadelphia, 1875. 2 vols.

Savage, John. *Our Living Representative Men.* Philadelphia, 1860.

Simms, Henry Harrison. *Life of Robert M. T. Hunter: A Study in Sectionalism and Secession.* Richmond, 1935.

Stephens, Alexander H. *A Constitutional View of the Late War Between the States; Its Causes, Character, Conduct and Results.* Philadelphia, 1868. 2 vols.

The War of the Rebellion: A Compilation of the Official Records of the Union and Confederate Armies. Washington, 1880-1901. 128 vols.

Wiltse, Charles M. *John C. Calhoun, Sectionalist, 1840-1850.* Indianapolis, 1951.

Wiley, Bell I. *The Life of Johnny Reb: The Common Soldier of the Confederacy.* Indianapolis, 1943.

Williams, T. Harry. *P. G. T. Beauregard: Napoleon in Gray.* Baton Rogue, 1954.

———. *Lincoln and His Generals.* New York, 1952.

Newspapers

Athens (Ga.) *Southern Banner,* 1860-1864; Athens (Ga.) *Southern Watchman,* 1868; Atlanta (Ga.) *Confederacy,* 1863; Augusta (Ga.) *Weekly Chronicle and Sentinel,* 1862-1865; *Daily Columbus* (Ga.) *Enquirer,* 1862-1863; Huntsville (Ala.) *Southern Democrat,* 1861; Milledgeville (Ga.) *Confederate Union* and *Southern Federal Union,* 1861-1865.

Index

A

Alabama, 13, 23, 26, 79, 81, 105, 130, 131
Americus, Ga., 94, 128
Anderson, Col. G. T., 56, 57, 58
Andersonville, Ga., 120, 122
Antietam, Battle of, 74
Apalachicola, Fla., 84
Apalachicola River, 79, 80, 81, 82, 83, 84, 85, 89
Army of the Peninsula, 40, 54
Army of the Potomac, 54, 72
Army of Northern Virginia, 66, 76, 77, 78
Army of Tennessee, 97, 103, 104, 106, 107, 121, 122
Athens, Ga., 13, 18, 21, 31, 41, 65, 67, 78, 79, 121, 122
Athens *Southern Banner*, 37
Athens *Southern Watchman*, 133
Atlanta, Ga., 31, 97, 98, 99, 100, 103, 104, 105, 106, 108, 121, 122, 123, 124, 125
Atlanta *Intelligencer*, 123
Augusta, Ga., 117, 120, 124, 128, 129
Augusta *Chronicle*, 130
Augusta *Constitutionalist*, 36
Augusta *Weekly Chronicle and Sentinel*, 123-124
Austria, 102

B

Bald Head, Camp, 124
Baldwin County, Ga., 78, 127
Baltimore, Md., 69
Barrow, Lt. James, 33, 34, 80, 81, 113
Beauregard, Gen. P. G. T., 76, 78, 79, 80, 81, 82, 83, 84, 85, 100, 104, 107, 108, 110, 116, 124 125, 126, 128, 129, 131
Bell, John, 18, 19
Benjamin, Sec. of War Judah P., 44, 63
Bibb County, Ga., 22
Black, Jeremiah S., 20

Bocock, Thomas, 51
Bragg, Gen. Braxton, 57, 97, 98, 99, 100, 102, 103, 104, 105, 106
Breckinridge, John C., 18, 19
Brockenborough, U. S. S., 84
Brown, Gov. Joseph E., 20, 21, 22, 29, 31, 37, 42, 77, 87, 89, 95, 98, 99, 100, 101, 111, 112 116, 117, 118, 119, 120, 121, 122, 123, 131
Browne, William M., 37, 39, 76, 86, 87, 90, 111
Brownsville Gap, Md., 71, 72
Bryan, Camp, 40
Bryan, Lt.-Col. Goode, 34, 44, 47
Buchanan, Pres. James, 13, 16, 17, 18, 19, 27, 43
Burnside, Gen. Ambrose E., 46, 49, 53

C

Calhoun, John C., 14
Cass, Lewis, 17
Central of Georgia Rail Road, 122
Charleston, S. C., 18, 50, 76, 78, 80, 82, 85, 124, 125
Charleston *Mercury*, 123
Chattahoochee, Fla., 80
Chattahoochee, C. S. S., 83
Chattahoochee River, 79, 82, 100, 131, 132
Chattanooga, Tenn., 97, 105
Chesapeake Bay, 46
Chickahominy River, 59, 60
Choctawhatchee River, 79, 81, 85, 86, 89
Clarke County, Ga., 19, 102
Clay, Henry, 14
Cleburne, Gen. Pat, 105, 106
Clover, Camp, 59
Cobb, Camp, 34, 37, 48
Cobb, Maj.-Gen. Howell, appearance, 13; birth, family, marriage, early career, 14; breaks with Democrats, 15; campaigns for Buchanan, 16; appointed Sec. of the Treas., 17; bid for presidential nomination, 18; favors secession in 1856, 19;

resigns from Buchanan's Cabinet, 20; works for secession, 21; hopes for peaceable secession, 22; helps take Georgia out of the Union, 23; elected president of Confederate Congress, 24; visits John Slidell, 27; presides over Congress, 28; opinion of Gov. Brown, 29; proposes to raise regiment, 30; speaks in Atlanta, 31; visits Sewall Point, Va., 32; begins recruiting regiment, 33; reports illness and deaths in regiment, 35-37; colonelcy approved, 38; view of Pres. Davis, 39, 49; supervises construction of fortifications, 40; adjusts to camp life, 41; visits ancestral estate, 42; view of *Trent* affair, 43-44; moves to new quarters, 45; view of Gen. Magruder, 46; torn between Richmond and Yorktown, 47; defeatism of, 48-49; advocates "scorched earth," 50; takes leave of Congress, 50-51; promoted to brigadier and predicts Lee's appointment, 52; heads Second Brigade, 53; movements of his brigade, 54; reports on morale of men, 55; Battle of Lee's Mill, 56-58; tells Yankee officer Richmond to be defended, 59; participates in fighting around Richmond, 60-62; illness of, 63; prisoner exchange talks, 63-65; reflections on war effort, 65; leads brigade into Maryland, 67-70; occupies Sandy Hook, Md., 71; disaster at Crampton's Gap, 72-74; activities after Battle of Crampton's Gap, 74-76; leaves Virginia, 76; transferred to Florida, 76-77; looks after his Georgia interests on way to Florida, 78; visits Beauregard, 79; speaks to Florida legislature, 80; inspects new district, 82; prepares defenses, 83-85; trouble with Yankee sailors, 84; advises Seddon, 86; view of conscript law, 87; troubles in Florida, 88-89; repulses Yankee raiders, 89-90; advised on treatment of Negro troops and addresses planters, 90; learns of brother's death, 91;

religious views and concern for wife, 92-94; sells provisions to Confederacy, 94; problem of his overseers, 95-96; social life in Quincy, 96; ordered to Atlanta, 97-98; quarrels with Gov. Brown, 101, 117-118; confers with Pres. Davis, 103; organized Georgia Guard, 99-100, 102-103; visits Bragg and assists Beauregard, 104; views after Missionary Ridge and Ringgold engagements, 105; displeased with Richmond, 107; promoted to major-general and leaves for Richmond, 106-107; urges invasion of Tennessee, 108-109; declines Florida post, 110; fails to save Guard, 109-110; contacts with the administration, 111; defends Davis, 112; death of his friend James Barrow, 113; establishes reserve headquarters in Macon, 115; problems in organizing reserve force, 116-119; reports progress in organizing reserve, 120-121; visits Gen. Johnston's headquarters, 121; directs Rebels at Battle of East Macon, 122; tours front with Davis, 124; advises Davis, 125; prepares to defend Macon against Sherman, 126; apprises Davis of low state of public morale, 127; fears Sherman will strike Southeast Georgia, 128; ordered to Alabama, 130; surrenders to Gen. Wilson, 132; opens law office in Macon, 132; death in New York, 132-133.
Cobb, Mrs. Howell, 33 36, 41, 58, 91, 92, 93, 96-97, 110, 128
Cobb, Howell, Jr., 28, 34, 68
Cobb, John A., 28, 32, 34, 35, 37, 55, 68, 77, 78, 94
Cobb, Lamar, 28, 32, 34, 68
Cobb, Mary Ann, 41
Cobb, Thomas, Jr., 92
Cobb, T. R. R. (Tom), 23, 34, 40, 41, 53, 56, 58, 63, 76, 91, 92
Coker, Lt. F. M., 70
Columbia, S. C., 20, 21
Columbus, Ga., 18, 79, 80, 81, 82, 100, 124, 131
Comfort, Camp, 60
Compromise of 1850, 14
Confederate Army, 30, 34, 37, 58, 71, 120

Holmes, Maj.-Gen. T. H., 54
Hood, Gen. John B., 122, 123, 124, 125, 127, 128, 129
Hunter, Sec. of State R. M. T., 47, 87

I

Illinois, 17
Iverson, Brig.-Gen. Alfred, 104, 105, 122

J

Jackson, Brig.-Gen. Henry Rootes, 50, 103, 104, 115, 116
Jackson, James, 37, 132
Jackson, Gen. "Stonewall," 71, 74
Jacksonians, 117, 118
Jacksonville, Fla., 90
James River, 54, 67
Jefferson, Thomas, 93
Johnston, Gen. Joseph E., 54, 58, 59, 60, 103, 107, 108, 120, 121, 122, 123, 126, 128, 129, 131
Jones, Gen. Sam, 117
Jonesboro, Ga., 123, 125

K

Kansas, 17
Kentucky, 52
Key, Col. Thomas M., 60, 64, 65
Kilcrease, Mrs. William E., 96, 97
Kilpatrick, Brig.-Gen. Judson, 125, 126
Know Nothing party, 16

L

Lamar, Camp, 45, 46, 48
Lamar, John B., 19, 22, 33, 34, 35, 36, 43, 74, 77, 78
Lee, Gen. Robert E., 52, 58, 60, 63, 64, 67, 69, 70, 74, 75, 76, 77 90, 107, 131
Lee's Mill, 56
Lee's Mill, Battle of, 56-58
Leesburg, Va., 69
Lincoln, Pres. Abraham, 17, 18, 19, 20, 21, 24, 43, 65, 112, 113
Lizzie, Camp, 75, 76
Logan, C. S. S., 39
London, 43
Longstreet, Gen. James, 76, 104, 108
Loring, Maj.-Gen. W. W., 53
Louisiana, 23, 27
Lovejoy's Station, Ga., 123, 124

M

Macon, Ga., 19, 22, 28, 30, 49, 78, 79, 94, 100, 106, 110, 120, 121, 122, 123, 124, 125, 126, 128, 129, 130, 132
Macon-Milledgeville Rail Road, 126
Magruder, Gen. John B., 35, 38, 40, 42, 45, 46, 47, 53, 54, 55, 56, 57, 58, 60
Malvern Hill, Battle of, 63, 65
Manassas, First Battle of, 34
Manassas, Second Battle of, 69
Martinsburg, Va., 75
Maryland, 24, 70, 71, 78, 92
Maryland Heights, 71, 73, 75
Mason, James M., 27, 28, 43
Mechanicsville Bridge, Va., 59
Memminger, Sec. of Treas. C. G., 44, 46, 47
Mercier, Count Henri, 27
Methodist Pulpit South, 93
Middle Florida, Military District of, 78, 79, 80, 81, 82, 88, 89, 91, 94, 97
Middletown, Md., 70
Military District of Georgia, 129
Military Division of the West, 124
Milton, Gov. John, 80, 81, 84, 87
Milton Dragoons, 84
Milledgeville, Ga., 14, 18, 121, 125, 126
Missionary Ridge, 105, 106
Mississippi, 23, 28, 131
Mobile, Ala., 81, 88
Monroe, Fort, 32, 35, 40, 54
Morehead City, N. C., 53
Moreno, Capt. Theodore, 79, 80, 83
Montgomery, Ala., 13, 23, 24, 28, 31, 131
Munford, Col. Thomas T., 72, 73, 75
McClellan, Gen. George B., 48, 54, 56, 57, 58, 59, 60, 63, 64, 65, 67, 72
McKinney Col. Robert M., 56
McLaws, Maj.-Gen. LaFayette, 39, 55, 67, 71, 72, 73, 75, 76-77, 116

N

Napoleon, Louis, 27
Norfolk, Va., 32, 53
North Carolina, 24, 52, 53
North Georgia, 103, 106, 117, 131
New Bern, N. C., 53
Newnan, Ga., 113
New Orleans, La., 13, 27